Cambridge Elements ≡

Elements in Publishing and Book Culture
Edited by
Samantha Rayner
University College London
Rebecca Lyons
University of Bristol

PUBLISHING AND THE SCIENCE FICTION CANON

FICTION CANON

The Case of Scientific Romance

Adam Roberts

Royal Holloway, University of London

CAMBRIDGE
UNIVERSITY PRESS

CAMBRIDGE
UNIVERSITY PRESS

University Printing House, Cambridge CB2 8BS, United Kingdom

One Liberty Plaza, 20th Floor, New York, NY 10006, USA

477 Williamstown Road, Port Melbourne, VIC 3207, Australia

314–321, 3rd Floor, Plot 3, Splendor Forum, Jasola District Centre,
New Delhi – 110025, India

79 Anson Road, #06–04/06, Singapore 079906

Cambridge University Press is part of the University of Cambridge.

It furthers the University's mission by disseminating knowledge in the pursuit of
education, learning, and research at the highest international levels of excellence.

www.cambridge.org
Information on this title: www.cambridge.org/9781108708890
DOI: 10.1017/9781108615648

© Adam Roberts 2019

This publication is in copyright. Subject to statutory exception
and to the provisions of relevant collective licensing agreements,
no reproduction of any part may take place without the written
permission of Cambridge University Press.

First published 2019

A catalogue record for this publication is available from the British Library.

ISBN 978-1-108-70889-0 Paperback
ISSN 2514-8524 (online)
ISSN 2514-8516 (print)

Cambridge University Press has no responsibility for the persistence or accuracy of
URLs for external or third-party internet websites referred to in this publication
and does not guarantee that any content on such websites is, or will remain,
accurate or appropriate.

Cambridge Elements

Publishing and the Science Fiction Canon

The Case of Scientific Romance

DOI: 10.1017/9781108615648

First published online: October 2018

Adam Roberts

Royal Holloway, University of London

ABSTRACT: Science fiction was being written throughout the seventeenth- and eighteenth-centuries, but it underwent a rapid expansion of cultural dissemination and popularity at the end of the nineteenth and beginning of the twentieth century. This Element explores the ways this explosion in interest in 'scientific romance', that informs today's global science fiction culture, manifests the specific historical exigences of the revolutions in publishing and distribution technology. H. G. Wells, Jules Verne and others science fiction writers embody in their art the advances in material culture that mobilise, reproduce and distribute with new rapidity, determining the cultural logic of twentieth-century science fiction in the process.

KEYWORDS: Literature, Science Fiction, Publishing

© Adam Roberts 2019

ISBNs: 9781108708890 (PB), 9781108615648 (OC)

ISSNs: 2514-8524 (online), 2514–8516 (print)

Contents

Publishing the Science Fiction Canon

Introduction

This Element is a small book about publishing and the canon of science fiction (SF). It concentrates on the later nineteenth and early twentieth centuries, although there are some excursions into later twentieth- and twenty-first-century SF. This small scope, however, entails some large problems. Both the question of what constitutes science fiction and the question of what we mean when talk about 'the canon' are complex and involved, and their mutual overlap here adds further eddies of complexity to the debate. Discussion here is mostly limited to the period reaching from the nineteenth century though to that literary periodisation known as Modernism, although I have elsewhere argued at length that science fiction starts considerably earlier (Roberts, *History of Science Fiction*).[1] Certainly it not only continues to grow after the Modernist period but expands exponentially into the twenty-first century. Since what I want to argue is that the material conditions of production of what is called 'scientific romance' determined key aspects of the form going forward, and therefore shaped important aspects of contemporary SF, what follows

---

[1] In my *History of Science Fiction*, I try to make the case that 'science fiction' as such separates from much longer-standing traditions of Fantastic storytelling and art around 1600 and suggest that the first SF novel is Kepler's *Somnium* (probably written *c.* 1600, although not published until 1632). My larger thesis is that SF is a cultural consequence of the Protestant Reformation, not in a strictly sectarian or religious-affiliative sense, but as an index of the way in which a new broadly materialist 'science' – from whence 'science fiction' in the modern sense becomes meaningful – emerges. My position on this remains an eccentric one where the community of science fiction scholarship is concerned: most critics who work in the field argue that SF 'begins' either in the nineteenth century or else – a less popular position – in the 1920s, when Hugo Gernsback coined the term 'science fiction'.

frequently looks forward to later works. The focus of this study, however, is largely last decades of the nineteenth century through to the First World War.

I have a thesis that I propose to develop, but I am of course conscious of the damage arbitrarily chosen parameters can do to the plausibility of an argument. To that end, I would like to start with some pointers. In terms of SF, there are two especially important centres of gravity around which almost all critical engagements with the mode have oriented themselves. One is Mary Shelley's *Frankenstein* (1818), which is often taken as the first SF novel. Brian Aldiss distinguishes it from previous stories containing fantastical elements because the central character 'makes a deliberate decision [and] turns' to 'modern experiments in the laboratory' in order to achieve his fantastic results (Aldiss, *Billion Year Spree*, p. 78). Contextually, Shelley's novel comes towards the end of the prominent vogue for Gothic fiction that began with Hugh Walpole's *The Castle of Otranto* (1764) and which had largely dissipated by the 1820s (see Hogle, *The Cambridge Companion to Gothic Fiction*).

The other 'centre of gravity' relevant here is the latter end of the century, and the rise to fame of two of science fiction's most prominent names: Frenchman Jules Verne, who published SF from *Voyage au centre de la Terre* (1864) through to his death in 1905; and Englishman H. G. Wells, whose debut novel *The Time Machine* appeared in 1895 and who continued publishing through to his death in 1946. These dates show that Verne and Wells come from different generations, and indeed the two men never met, even though their reputations are strangely interwoven.

It is from the 1880s, and especially the 1890s, that we can date the expansion of SF, its shift from being a niche form of cultural production, with small print runs, limited readerships and a marginal place in publishing, through a rapid commercial expansion based around cheaper books, and (especially) magazines – 'Pulps' – into cinema and TV and, finally, to our present state of affairs, in which SF and Fantasy, especially in 'Young Adult' (YA) writing and superhero modes, has a greater cultural penetration, and flat outsell all other forms of cultural production.[2] The period under consideration here, in other words, figures as a hinge point in the larger narratives of genre.

In between these two broadly indicative points of chronology, Shelley at the beginning of the century and Verne-Wells at the end, anglophone and francophone book publishing developed in several key ways. Of course, limiting myself to the British and French traditions is another selectivity that needs to be acknowledged. In a book of this scope, one cannot cover everything, and although there were important SF traditions developing in other cultures – especially in Poland, Spain, Italy and of course the United States – by the beginning of the twentieth-century, SF as a genre had, largely speaking, yet to take hold in South and East Asia, South America or in Africa. Many Russian readers spoke French – Hetzel, Verne's publisher, applied pressure to change the text of *Vingt mille lieues sous les mer* (*Twenty Thousand Leagues Under the Sea*, 1869–70), shifting the motivation of his submariner Captain Nemo from an anti-Russian to an anti-British stance so as not to alienate his large Russian readership (see Martin, *The Mask of the Prophet*). The most widely translated and best-selling fiction in Russia between the 1860s and the 1930s were the works of Verne, Walter Scott and to a lesser extent those of Conan Doyle and Wells (Ruud, *Russian Entrepreneur*). In other words, these were writers who were read across the world, as well as writers

---

[2] On the rise of SF as a cultural idea, see Westfahl, *The Mechanics of Wonder*. On the Pulps, see Ashley, *The Time Machines*. My *History of Science Fiction* (Roberts, *History of Science Fiction*, pp. 479–512) provides some data to support the claims about today's dominance of SF and Fantasy, although few today can be blind to the extraordinary contemporary success of the *Star Wars* franchise, the Marvel Comics Universe movies and spin-offs and the *Harry Potter* series, as well as the many Young Adult dystopias.

who had a direct impact on the way in which the genre developed through the twentieth century. So whilst the English- and French-language foci of this study is limiting and even to a degree distorting, they may not be *fatally* distorting. Given that one of the aims of this study is to explore the ways the practical specificities of book production in nineteenth-century SF fed through into the broader cultural logic of the mode then *and* now, it will be important to keep an eye on continuities.

Across the century, then, many thousands of SF books and stories were published, and from that larger body it is possible, by triangulating contemporary popularity and latter-day critical interest, to hypothecate a potential 'canon' of nineteenth-century SF. It is worth doing this in order to make plain the sorts of assumptions the underpin the argument being developed in this study (the meaning of the term 'canon' is explored in more detail later; for more detailed discussion see Gorak, *The Making of the Modern Canon*).

Observations of the 'such a list can never pretend to objectivity' kind are rendered supernumerary by their very obviousness. Still, and even though it might easily be augmented, or even, with more difficulty (I think) reduced, I am going to set out the following list of titles. We could hardly omit Mary Shelley's *Frankenstein* (1818). I shall also add E. T. A. Hoffman's *Der Sandmann* (1817), the first story of an automated human, which would later come to be called a 'robot', as well as Auguste Villiers de l'Isle-Adam's *L'Éve Future* (1886), which is a celebrated, though more misogynist, later iteration of the same idea; Adam Seaborn's hollow-earth fantasia, *Symzonia* (1820), which was taken as fact by some; Jane Loudon's *The Mummy! A Tale of the Twenty-Second Century* (1827), the first 'Egyptian mummy' novel; Louis-Napoléon Geoffroy's *Napoléon et la conquête du monde* (1836, revised as *Napoléon Apocryphe* in 1841), detailing Napoleon's defeat of Russia and conquest of the whole globe, generally taken to be the first 'alternate history' novel; the various works of Edgar Allan Poe, especially perhaps the cod-lunar adventure,

'The Unparalleled Adventure of Hans Pfaall' (1835) and the mysterious voyage tale, *Narrative of Arthur Gordon Pym* (1838); Charlemagne Ischir Defontenay's *Star, ou Psi de Cassiopée* (1854), a story of humanoid aliens living in the constellation of Cassiopeia, taken by some to be the first space opera; *Achille Eyraud's* interplanetary adventure, *Voyage à Venus* (1866); Edward Bulwer Lytton's *The Coming Race* (1871) about superhumans living underground whose advanced society is powered by a force called 'vril', from which the beef-spread Bovril took its name; astronomer Camille Flammarion's interstellar sense-of-wonder masterpieces, *Lumen* (1872), *Stella* (1877) and *Uranie* (1889), Albert Robida's trilogy of lavishly-illustrated futuristic extrapolations, *Le Vingtième Siècle* (1883), *La Guerre au vingtième siècle* (1887), *Le Vingtième siècle: la vie électrique* (1890) and Edwin Abbott's brief, mathematical fantasia, *Flatland* (1884). These books enjoyed modest print-runs, and appealed to a relatively small early-century reading public.

The question of popularity is germane, since around the time the latter few titles listed above were published there was a distinct step-change in the level of popularity of SF. Somewhere around the 1870s and 1880s, a post-*Frankenstein* body of cultural production began to 'take off' commercially, in both Britain and France, buoyed by the general increase in publishing volume, readerly competence and disposable income.[3] Jules Verne's career began slowly – 1863's *Cinq semaines en ballon* (*Five Weeks in a Balloon*) and 1864's *Voyages et aventures du capitaine Hatteras* (*Voyages and Adventures of Captain Hatteras*) were modest commercial successes – but by the 1870s he had become

---

[3] 'In the early years of the nineteenth century, novels were rarely produced in print runs of more than 1000 or 1500 copies. By the 1840s editions of 5000 copies were more common, while in the 1870s the cheapest editions of Jules Verne appeared in editions of 30,000 and were often reprinted' (Lyons, 'New Readers in the Nineteenth Century', p. 341). See also Lyons, *Readers and Society in Nineteenth-century France*.

one of the best-selling writers in the world. His breakthrough work, *Vingt mille lieues sous les mers: Tour du monde sous-marin* (*Twenty Thousand Leagues Under the Seas: A Tour of the Underwater World*) was serialised 1869–70, and sold especially well in its 1871 octavo reissue. Verne's reputation and sales built steadily through the 1870s and 1880s (Butcher, *Jules Verne*).

And Verne was not alone. Marie Corelli's melodramatic work of space-spiritualism, *The Romance of Two Worlds* (1889) became one of the century's best-selling titles, despite being a notably poor piece of writing.[4] George Tomkyns Chesney's short novel of a future German invasion of the UK, *The Battle of Dorking* (1871), was a huge hit and became a political talking point: after appearing first in Blackwood's magazine it created such demand that the issue in which it appeared had to be reprinted six times; issued as a sixpenny paperback volume, it sold an unprecedented 20,000 copies a week. Similarly in the US, Edward Bellamy's utopian future extrapolation, *Looking Backward 2000–1887* (1888) galvanised a movement. Bellamy's book was a phenomenon: it sold in the millions. Indeed, in the whole American nineteenth century, only *Uncle Tom's Cabin* (1852) and *Ben-Hur* (1880) sold more copies than *Looking Backward* – and had a direct impact on American society. Over 150 'Bellamy Clubs' to discuss the book's ideas were formed, and a new 'Nationalist' political party was established to contest the Presidency. In literary terms it inspired a whole genre of future-extrapolated utopias and dystopias, amongst them William Morris's *News From Nowhere* (1890) and H. G. Wells's *When The Sleeper Wakes* (1899).

Edward Everett Hale's *The Brick Moon* (1869–70) cannot match these titles for sales, but often appears in histories of SF as the first work about a man-

---

[4] Annette Frederico notes that 'on average a Corelli novel sold 100,000 copies a year' in the 1880s, a figure that had risen to '175,000 copies a year' by the turn of the century (Frederico, *Idol of Suburbia*, p. 2).

made orbital satellite. And indeed, works often become 'canonical' in terms of the history of SF because they are taken to be the first iteration of something that would prove important in later SF. Much of Wells's own *oeuvre* figures in this way: his *The Time Machine* (1895) still has the best claim to be the first work about time travel as a practicable, material business; *The Island of Doctor Moreau* (1896) is the first work to relocate the talking beasts of fairy tale and fable into the idiom of science (or pseudo-science); *The War of the Worlds* (1898) is the first and still one of the best accounts of alien invasion, and the aforementioned *When The Sleeper Wakes* (1899) put in play a whole range of conventions about future dystopia.[5] Another marker of cultural influence, and therefore of canonicity, is the number of adaptations to stage, film, TV and other media of any given title. Wells scores highly, so to speak, by this criterion, as do some, though by no means all, of Verne's many titles: the subterranean *Voyage au centre de la Terre* (1864), submarine *Vingt Mille Lieues sous les mers* (1869–70) and globe-spanning *Le Tour du monde en quatre-vingts jours* (1872) have all been many times adapted. In terms of commercial success and cultural penetration, Verne and Wells vie with one another for dominance in terms of the development of science fiction going forward.

This sketched-out canon of nineteenth-century SF is not likely to be particularly controversial. Matters become harder to narrow down as we move through the twentieth century and the river of textual production broadens and deepens into a swift-moving delta of interconnected sub-genres and styles. Historians of the genre talk of the age of 'Pulps' (broadly the 1920s and 1930s),

---

[5] Mark Hillegas argues that *Sleeper* provides the basic template for subsequent iterations of this kind of story with a whole series of now-familiar story-props, conceits and settings: 'the enclosed super-city, the disappearance of the family, the elimination of privacy, the degradation of the working class, the use of "kine-tele-photography" and "babble machines" for propaganda, pleasure cities, euthanasia, and mental surgery' (Hillegas, *The Future as Nightmare*, p. 108).

the 'Golden Age' of the 1940s and 1950s, the 'New Wave' of the 1960s and 1970s, but these are broad brush attempts at categorisation, incapable of apprehending the explosion in the variety of work being produced. These works are both 'high-brow/literary' as pulp, as likely to be visual texts – comic books, films, TV, latterly video games – as verbal ones. By the time we reach the 1980s, extending right to the present day, critics can do no better than gesture towards prominent subgenres within the larger logic according to which SF frames cultural production as a whole – cyberpunk, YA, superheroes, alt-history, military SF, dystopia. In short, SF has become, by the 20-teens, a climate rather than a focused genre.

This study cannot follow the development of the genre too far into this intriguing contemporary fecundity. Its ambition is, by contract, almost risibly modest: to argue that one iteration of SF's protean variety, known to critics as the 'scientific romance', is as much an artefact of a shift in the underlying logic of commercial publication at the very end of the nineteenth century and beginning of the twentieth, as it is anything else. I shall argue, in other words, that scientific romance flourishes during a particular hiatus, after the older dominance of circulating libraries had become largely obsolete but before the newer commercial restrictions of the Net Book Agreement had come into force. I shall stress, furthermore, that this state of affairs is not a coincidence, rather that the form of this type of SF actually directly expresses that underlying cultural-economic substrate. In some sense, this window, shaped by a set of particular exigences to do with the manufacture and sale of fiction, generated the 'scientific romance' as we now understand it.

One qualifier might be added, which is that if this thesis is a correct assessment of the determining forces of 'scientific romance', then a corollary follows: if these social and cultural circumstances proved, albeit indirectly, so very important for the way SF evolved through the twentieth century, then it is clear that the material circumstances of book production and reception in the later nineteenth century feed directly through into the later development of genre.

How these matters interact with the questions of the 'canon' are also complex. Preferring one text to another as a possible member of a canon of 'classics' or 'important works' inevitably constitutes the erection of a hierarchy. In the case of SF, this brute truth manifests on two levels: in-genre and metagenerically. To prefer a selection of (for the sake of argument) straight white male authors as canonical over, let us say, a selection of queer female writers of colour is to reinscribe inside genre the larger malign hierarchies of worth that structure society as a whole, and as such is surely to be deplored. The SF and Fantasy Writers of America organisation appoints certain highly regarded writers as 'Grandmasters', not 'Grandmistresses', while Victor Gollancz's series of canonical SF novels are published under the rubric 'Masterworks', nor 'Mistressworks'. These may seem trivial infractions, but at least indicate that the nomenclature of in-genre canonicity is not neutral.

Of course, *any* selection, by silencing some voices and preferring others, is in a sense prejudicial. And the series of choices that arrive eventually as the canon within science fiction replicates a larger-grained exercise that happens between genres, where 'literary fiction', 'serious poetry', 'drama' (or some of it) is preferred to debased and populist 'genre' writing such as Science Fiction, Romance Fiction, Crime and the Western. This latter cleavage opens up properly in the twentieth century, when a group of arbiters of taste strove to establish a canon of literature as such, and that high-status, academically endorsed body of literary experimentation across a variety of modes called Modernism is sharply distinguished from mere 'reading-matter', that extruded entertainment product of Pulp and genre writing, which is dismissed as inartistic pabulum. That figures as different as Q. D. Leavis and Theodor

Adorno can be bracketed together in this respect speaks to the intellectual incoherence, or at least the conceptual *oddity*, of this approach.

In fact 'High Modernism' (as the movement is sometimes called) is just as penetrated by science fiction as are more popular modes like dime novels and Pulp magazines. This is a claim about more than the obvious titles – Huxley's *Brave New World*, Hesse's *Das Glasperlenspie* – where scholars and teachers of Modernism may begrudgingly concede room on their syllabi for unusual examples of SF. It is also a claim about Modernism itself, a movement radically determined by its fascinations with technology, time, new modes of apprehending space and the 'make it new' logic of the novum. What is *À la recherche du temps perdu* if it is not a time-travel story?

This argument perhaps runs the risk of appearing merely polemical, not least because the narrative of split between 'High Art' and 'popular culture' is so ingrained in the way we look at the twentieth century. Mozart can compose crowd-pleasing musical spectacles like *Die Zauberflöte*; Dickens can be the Victorian period's most popular entertainer and a conscious artist in the novel form; but as the twentieth century develops, artistry and popularity part company. There is another sort of canonicity in this fact, too. But before proceeding to examine this, more clarity is required to explain and theorise what 'canonicity' means for the purposes of the current study.

Notes on the Concept of a Canon

The science fiction canon proposed earlier lists a tiny percentage of the thousands of separate works of SF that were published throughout the nineteenth century, almost all of which have fallen into readerly desuetude, remembered if at all by specialist bibliographers and completists in search of the obscurities of genre. To say so is to approach a thumbnail definition of the 'canon' as such, of course. Whatever else it is, the canon is what is left over when the majority of cultural production has been excluded – or, if one prefers, when a small sample of all cultural production has been selected. The justification for the canon that comes closest to neutrality of statement is the following: 'after all, one cannot read *everything* . . . ' although no critic have ever claimed that this process of selection, or exclusion, can be a wholly innocent one. Historically it has been the case that male writers and white writers have tended to be selected, while women writers and writers of colour have tended to be excluded. Some attempts to reverse this prejudicial climate of literary canonisation have been undertaken in many schools and university departments over the last few decades, by ensuring that women and writers of colour are included in syllabi alongside, as the phrase goes, the 'dead white males' (Kolbas, *Critical Theory and the Literary Canon*; Morrissey, *Debating the Canon*). But although it would not be true to say that school and university teaching has *no* impact on the larger cultural profile of the canon, it is hard to deny that canons as *cultural* formations tend to be bottom-up, rather than top-down, phenomena. Hubris is a harsh word to apply to a group of mostly perfectly well-meaning people, but the notion that a brace of university-level courses can undo the structuring sexism and racism of culture as such is, at the very least, over-optimistic. John Guillory (*Cultural Capital*, p. 6) makes the point that the terminology of 'canonicity' has replaced the older language of 'classics' 'precisely in order to isolate the "classics" as the object of critique'. He also argues that critics' 'telegraphic invocation of race/class/gender' – which is, I concede, exactly what I am doing here – merely indicates 'the failure to develop a systemic analysis that would integrate the distinctions and nuances of social theory into the practice of canonical revision' (p. 11). Though the present study lacks the dimensions to permit such integration, its attempt to situate its proposed nineteenth-century SF canon in terms of the material production of certain kinds of texts and certain forms of social access is, at least in part, a response to Guillory's critique.

In the case of science fiction there are distinct levels by which specifically SF texts fit into this larger critical narrative of canonicity. On the level of individual texts, SF has developed own canon, both in the top-down university syllabus sense (so it is that Ursula Le Guin, Margaret Atwood and Octavia Butler are widely taught at tertiary level) and in the bottom-up sense of an active and engaged fandom. On the level of genres or modes of writing as such, institutional respect for SF has mapped the broader, and sometimes, grudging opening of English Literature departments to the study of 'popular culture' as such. As noted earlier, SF both internalises and, in toto, embodies the problematics of the canon.

In addition to representing a selection of texts made for the purposes of pedagogy, or for cultural preeminence and control, the canon can also be thought of as *those texts which a person with pretentions to cultural literacy would be ashamed to admit they did not know.* I mean 'pretentions to cultural literacy' both in the general sense – the aspirations of that sort of person who wishes to be seen as broadly *au fait* with the best that has been thought and known (to appropriate Matthew Arnold's definition of culture) – but also in a more specific sense, as proof of membership of one or other in-groups, the quasi-tribal shibboleths that mark an individual as, let us say, a classical music buff, or an aficionado of Victorian literature – or a fan of SF. A classical music buff would be ashamed to admit they had never heard a Beethoven symphony, but would feel less shame in confessing ignorance of the operas of eighteenth-century Milanese composer, Giovanni Battista Lampugnani. This is a way of saying that Beethoven's music belongs to the canon of classical music in a way that Lampugnani's does not – this is of course not to say that the latter's music is worthless or contemptible, only that there does not exist the cultural pressure to acquaint oneself with it if one wishes to be considered 'knowledgeable' about classical music. We could make similar arguments about (say) Elisabeth Gaskell and

George Eliot as canonical to the Victorian novel in ways not true of Frederick Marryat or Marie Corelli – though both were extremely popular in their own day, and in fact considerably outsold Gaskell and Eliot.

Were I, as a critic and historian of the genre and as a university teacher (and I belong to both groups), to offer a course in SF, it would be merely perverse of me to draw up a syllabus that preferred Thomas Erskine's *Armata* (1817), which is about a second Earth connected to our world via a south polar umbilicus, over Mary Shelley's *Frankenstein* (1818). And as a fan I would be ashamed to admit ignorance of the latter, but not of the former. Likewise, to move to the end of the century, Verne's SF works are canonical in, as it were, both directions when compared to Louis Boussenard's *Dix mille ans dans un bloc de glace* (*10,000 Years in a Block of Ice*, 1890). Wells's novels are simply more canonical than Francis Worcester Doughty's *Mirrikh, or A Woman from Mars: a Tale of Occult Adventure* (1892). The top-down and the bottom-up can arrive at a consensus that creates the sorts of territory that might, with a degree of consensus, be labelled canon.

Scientific Romance

One last example of, as it were, critical throat-clearing is needed before I move on to the meat of my argument: a word on the definition of 'scientific romance' itself. As a piece of critical terminology it has, surprisingly perhaps, a rather wide range of applications. It is a term that itself comes out of the middle of the nineteenth century. The earliest usages unearthed by scholarship include the following:

> Charles Dickens's description [24 March 1866 *All the Year Round*] of Henri de Parville's *Un habitant de la planète Mars: roman*

d'anticipation (1865); and James de Mille's *A Strange Manuscript Found in a Copper Cylinder* (*Harper's Weekly*; 1888), where a character in the Club-Story frame describes the manuscript's tale as scientific romance. C H Hinton issued two series of *Scientific Romances* (1886 and 1898) mixing speculative essays and stories, and the term was widely applied by reviewers and essayists to the early novels of H G Wells, which became the key exemplars of the genre. (Stapleford et al., *Scientific Romance*)

Critic and writer Brian Stableford revived the term in the later twentieth century in order to distinguish between what he considers a distinctive European tradition in SF from the eventually dominant American tradition. Stableford's *Scientific Romance in Britain 1890–1950* (1985) contrasts what he argues are more downbeat British scientific romances, often texts that engage with long evolutionary timescales, or technologies of scale that dwarf the protagonist, with the more up-beat action-adventure can-do individualised frontier heroism of the American tradition, the latter form coming to prevail over the genre more generally with the success of the Pulps in the 1920s and 1930s. It might look from the title of his monograph that Stableford has a wider chronological understanding of the range of works that can usefully be described as scientific romances than is assumed by the present study. In fact, although Stableford notes that 'although it does make perfect sense to employ *roman scientifique* and scientific romance as a descriptive term for material published after 1918, especially in Britain and France', he concedes that 'there is a sense in which the genre [had] lost its impetus' by the 1920s, when the 'American notion of "science fiction"' made inroads 'prior to the Second World War' (Stapleford, *Scientific Romance*, p. xi). The present study defines the chronological scope of the scientific romance around the last two decades of the nineteenth century and the first two of the twentieth.

One way of looking at this question is to examine those later twentieth- and twenty-first century works of SF that attract the description, 'scientific romance', because they are indulging in a nostalgic or retro-aesthetic engagement with the props, tropes or sometimes just the mood of SF from 1880–1920. The vogue for this began in the 1970s, with works such as Michael Moorcock's *The Warlord of the Air* (1971) and Harry Harrison's *A Transatlantic Tunnel Hurrah!* (1972), an Edwardian-set adventure written in a pastiche of the style of that time, and filled with the sorts of 'advanced' technology – warships, steam-powered machinery – that might have struck the futuristic note in 1900 but which now look quaintly alt-historical. A later, more directly intertextual example of the same thing is Christopher Priest's Wellsian midrash *The Space Machine* (1976), a novel that combines elements from *The Time Machine* and *The War of the Worlds* into a more technologically advanced alt-historical 1890s. As an increasing number of similar stories were published, a collective version of late Victorian and Edwardian Britain coalesced into what is nowadays a vibrant and widely popular subgenre of SF: steampunk. The success of this emergent subgenre was cemented by William Gibson and Bruce Sterling's popular *The Difference Engine* (1990), set in a version of the Victorian age in which Charles Babbage's proto-computer 'difference engine' has been made to work and has revolutionised technology; this work created a new climate in genre. It quickly had many imitators, and by the twenty-first century had become a stylistically distinct mode not only of literature and visual art but also of SF fandom itself. The hospitality of this 'scientific-romantic' aesthetic to fan engagement is a main reason why it has proved an enduring in-genre.[6]

---

[6] Scores of 'steampunk' novels and stories continue to be published annually. Samples run the gamut from the pulpiest of the Pulp to the work of a literary heavyweight like Thomas Pynchon, than whom few are (in a literary sense) heavier, and whose huge

'Steampunk' cosplay – dressing up in Victorian styles augmented with technological adornment – is especially popular.[7]

The point of this is to indicate the extent to which contemporary SF remains somewhat in love with an elegant pseudo-Victorian or Edwardian version of their SF world making. It remains in commercial terms a minor rather than a major iteration of SF, but it is an important one, and it crystallises some of the key elements – the *sorts* of technology, the style of (as it might be) aircraft, spacecraft, time machines and so on, a prevailing mood – that are

steampunk fantasia, *Against the Day* (2006), may be his masterpiece. There are many steampunk-style video games: *BioShock Infinite* (2K Games: 2013) for instance, which sold over eleven million copies, or the older *Myst* series of games (until 2002 this series was the world's best-selling video game). Films as diverse as the Japanese animé, *Hauru no Ugoku Shiro* (*Howl's Moving Castle*, Hayao Miyazaki, 2004) and the Hollywood reboot *Sherlock Holmes* (Guy Ritchie, 2009) embody steampunk stylings. It has proved a particularly fruitful area for YA writing, with many of the novels of Philip Pullman, including the *His Dark Materials* trilogy (*Northern Lights* (1995), *The Subtle Knife* (1997), *The Amber Spyglass* (2000)), the work of Philip Reeve, especially his *Mortal Engines* quartet (2001–06) and American author Cassandra Clare and her *Infernal Devices* trilogy (*Clockwork Angel* (2010), *Clockwork Prince* (2011), *Clockwork Princess* (2013)). *Doctor Who*, whose protagonist is in effect an Edwardian gentleman in possession of a spaceship, can be thought of as, in essence, a steampunk show. Though the focus of this literature is often a version of Victorian England, it has also proved very popular abroad, with works like the *Trilogía Victoriana* of Spanish writer, Félix J Palma (*El mapa del tiempo* (2008), *El mapa del tiempo* (2012), *El mapa del caos* (2014)), or Frenchman Jean-Christophe Valtat's powerful *Aurorarama* (2010). The reconstituted 'scientific romance' continues to play a vigorous part in contemporary SF. A good overview of the mode is provided by Vandermeer and Chambers (*The Steampunk Bible*).

[7] A number of works are in print that offer guidance on how to 'perform' steampunk, with advice on dress, accessories and so on. See for example, Hewitt, *Steampunk Emporium*; Marsocci and DeBlasio, *How to Draw Steampunk*.

relevant to a study of the scientific romance in context. It is, we might argue, a form of pervasive nostalgia within science fiction for a more elegant age. There is, in other words, an interesting contradiction, or at least the appearance of a contradiction, at the heart of the contemporary vogue for steampunk: SF, that rebus for modernity, most famous for its iterations of futurity, contains within it a yearning for a past – but a past that never actually existed. This is less of a paradox than it might seem. As Agnes Heller ('Cultural Memory, Identity and Civil Society') has persuasively argued, the logic of modernity inevitably contains within it an, as it were, corrective nostalgia for a past, remedially addressing the anxieties of an uncertain future with an ideologically over-determined version of past surety. 'Every generation,' Heller notes, 'experiences the past as their present', with the twist that cultural discourse overwrites the quiddity of the past with its symptomatic function. 'We know that Caesar was not murdered on the Capitolium,' is her example, 'but when we visit the Capitolium in Rome we – readers of Plutarch and of Shakespeare – will visit the place were Caesar was murdered' (p. 139).

This is one explanation for the peculiar lineaments of steampunk, the persistence of 'the scientific romance' into twenty-first century SF. 'Our' nostalgia, as science fiction fans, is for a form of SF that retains those elements of the genre that we prize, the sense of wonder, the expansive and even transcendental possibilities, but retrofits them into a more elegant, more mannerly and – inevitably – more ideologically conservative past world.[8] Nostalgia is, amongst other things, a process of selection and prioritisation; it

---

[8] 'Nostalgic conceptions of the past contribute to a tacit acceptance of the status quo (including, for examples, unmarked privileges associated with whiteness, masculinity, bourgeois backgrounds and heterosexuality) . . . the present interprets the past, and, in this process, certain meanings of the past are chosen for emphasis while other meanings are excluded' (Wilson, *Nostalgia*, p. 45).

functions, on the level of collective memory, as precisely the way canon formation functions on the level of textual production.

This, though, is to treat the subject from one angle only: the present, looking backward. Inflected by this vector though it inevitably is, the specific argument of this study runs the other way, from the past to the present: the ways in which the logic of book-production, publishing, distribution and readership of the later nineteenth and early twentieth century shaped the subsequent development of SF. And to that the argument now turns.

The Nineteenth-Century Book Market

Properly to understand the 'canon' sketched at the head of this study, we need to have some sense of the publishing context that shaped the production of the works out of which it is constituted. Speaking broadly, there are three especially important ways in which book production changed between the era of Shelley's *Frankenstein* and that of Verne's *Vingt mille lieues sous les mers* and Wells's *War of the Worlds*. First, it expanded massively; second, its unit costs shrank remarkably; and third, its products became considerably secularised in terms of content (for a good summary of this large and complex topic, see Eliot, 'Some Trends in British Book Production 1800–1919'). This means that the books published at the beginning of the nineteenth-century were (by modern standards) few, expensive and limited in topic, which a high preponderance of religious titles. The majority of books were religious – collections of sermons, commentaries on the Bible and the like.[9] Of course many individual works of fiction were produced, and

---

[9] Just limiting ourselves to sermons alone, and not considering the many works of Biblical commentary, instruction, theology, religious allegory (and, of course, actual Bibles), Jennifer Farooq calculates that 'sermons accounted for as many as one in

some of those had a wide readership; but the *relative* importance of the novel form, and its dedicated readership, grew exponentially towards the century's end, as developments in the material production of books met the much larger reading public created by reformation in public education.

This latter fact is the horizon within which all book production necessarily exists: books, after all, cannot be sold to an illiterate audience. The UK Parliament passed a number of Elementary Education Acts between 1870 and 1893, and these vastly increased levels of literacy amongst the general population. In 1840, less than two-thirds of grooms and less than half of brides in England and Wales could sign their own names at marriage; in 1900, 97 per cent of both groups could do so (fully functional literacy, sufficient for reading novels for pleasure, would have been lower in both cases of course, but these numbers give a sense of the magnitude of the social shift). Similar moves in France reduced the percentages of illiteracy from 53 per cent of men and 73 per cent of women in 1790 to 23 per cent of men and 33 per cent of women in 1876. By 1900, both numbers were in the low single figures (Woods, *The Demography of Victorian England and Wales*; Furet and Ozouf, *Lire et écrire: l'alphabétisation des français de Calvin à Jules Ferry*).

These two forces, the much larger production of considerably cheaper books and the massive increase in the numbers of people able to read and desirous of doing so, created a wholly new reading culture in Europe. But these two brute forces must be understood via a third: the means by which books were distributed to readers. For much of the century, distribution in Britain and France was dominated by lending libraries. The expensiveness of books, market-determined in the eighteenth and early nineteenth centuries, was

every fourteen titles,' published in the eighteenth century, 'which meant that about two or three sermons a week came off the presses' (Farooq, *Preaching in Eighteenth-Century London*, p. 74).

artificially maintained through the century's middle decades and gave those libraries extraordinary power in mediating market dynamics and public demand to determine the sorts of books that were available, and so shape literary culture significantly.

Nineteenth-century lending libraries were not free. On the contrary, they charged often quite large annual fees. Borrowers tended to be middle class and respectable: the very wealthy could afford to amass their own collections of books, and 'working men's libraries', paid for by charitable institutions or nascent labour collectives, tended to stock practical and 'useful' books rather than fiction. In Britain, the influence of libraries on nineteenth-century literary culture was considerable. The biggest was Mudie's Select Library, established by Charles Edward Mudie in 1842. In this institution, an annual subscription of one guinea (£1 1s) entitled the reader to borrow one volume at a time, where a five-guinea subscription allowed the reader to borrow up to six volumes at a time.[10] The stipulation was *volumes*, not complete novels. The habit of publishing Victorian novels as 'triple-deckers', in three separately bound portions, enabled Mudie's to lend one novel to three separate readers at any given time, and so triple his income. This fact, combined with an aggressive pricing strategy that discouraged the private purchase of such fiction, embedded the triple-decker as the mainstay of mid-Victorian publishing. Guinevere L. Griest (*Mudie's Circulating Library and the Victorian Novel*) shows how it worked: Mudie's market power was such that he could compel

---

[10] For comparison, the average UK worker's wage in the later nineteenth century was £42 14s, or about £3 10s a month. Five guineas is, clearly, a large sum in relation to this. A guinea a week was considered a small but respectable – that is, barely a middle-class – income. The much greater disparity between rich and poor of the nineteenth century meant that the wealthy subsisted on vastly more than these sums, of course (figures from Bowley, *Wages in the United Kingdom in the Nineteenth-Century*).

publishers to price their novels artificially high: typically 31s 6d for three volumes (his library bought the same novels at the discount price of 15s; if publishers baulked, he did not buy their stock at all); Mudie's thereby discouraged generations of nineteenth-century British readers from buying their own copies of the novels they read. It became, as Griest shows, an axiom of publishing at this time that the British were simply not a book-buying people. Griest gives various examples: whereas *Moby Dick* sold in America for $1.50, it cost the equivalent of $7.80 when it appeared as *The Whale* in Great Britain.

Mudie's and a few others operated what amounted to a stranglehold on the British book market through the middle decades of the century. This, though, was not destined to last. Two factors in particular eroded the importance of the circulating libraries. One was the emergence of public circulating libraries: a series of Public Libraries Acts 1850–68 began, slowly, to create free-to-access libraries in the UK, beginning with facilities in Birmingham and Manchester. The other was a shift in publishing towards 'cheap' editions, less lavishly produced and sold for shillings rather than pounds. For a while, Mudie's was able to impose on publishers an interval of one year between the appearance of the triple-decker and any cheaper edition, but as the century went on the taste for triple-deckers shifted to one-volume works, and the power of Mudie's and its ilk waned.

In France, no one library dominated the French book market in the way that Mudie's had in Britain, but Graham Falconer ('Provincial Circulating Libraries in Nineteenth-Century France') has shown how powerful and deter-mining libraries nonetheless were to French reading habits. In addition to lending out titles for a fee, French libraries often encompassed ancillary businesses as printers, stationers and bookbinders, and this effectively meant that they worked as de facto arbiters of taste, especially with respect to the cultural tension between popular *romans* and the more elite category of *littérature*.[11] Falconer also shows that in France the influence of the libraries waned sharply in the second half of the century as cheaper forms of book production and new modes of distribution and sales changed the country's book-buying landscape.

In other words, a large portion of the nineteenth-century literary culture in both Britain and France was dominated by the circulating libraries, which in turn shaped the sorts of books that reached readers. One important aspect of this was the creation of a literary 'mainstream', against which a set of effective 'margins' might be defined. It is fair to say that SF, as a genre, has been consistently located in the latter conceptual space; arguably, this very identification is a product of this period. In Britain the triple-decker functioned as the default of literary production, and books originally issued in that format remain canonical in (for example) university English departments – the major works of Walter Scott, Charles Dickens, George Eliot, Charlotte and Emily Brontë, Joanna Trollope and William Thackeray were all issued in this manner, and almost without exception these novels were mimetic narratives, either historical or more-or-less contemporaneous with an emphasis on the interactions of a cast of relatable characters: courtship, friendships, family and interfamilial tensions and so on. They were, in a nutshell, designed to appeal to that respectable bourgeois readership with disposable income amongst whom library subscriptions were common. When Mudie's refused to carry a title – as it did with, as one example, George Moore's novels – it was usually on grounds of indecency, indexing a disinclination to alienate its middle-class subscribers (Moore, furious, published two tracts attacking the dominance of circulating libraries: *Literature at Nurse* and *Circulating Morals*, both 1885).

---

[11] The standard work on French lending libraries in the nineteenth century remains Parent-Lardeur (*Lire à Paris au temps de Balzac*) upon which Falconer's essay expands.

George Gissing's *New Grub Street* draws on Gissing's own experience as a struggling writer in the 1880s. That novel's gifted but oversensitive protagonist, Edwin Reardon, forces his writing gifts into the procrustean bed of the triple-decker and so ruins his own art. A friend, also a writer, offers him advice: 'I gravely advise people, if they possibly can, to write of the wealthy middle class; that's the popular subject, you know.' Reardon tries, but the difficulties inherent in the form defeat him: 'the critics,' Gissing's narrator says, 'are wont to point out the weakness of second volumes; they are generally right, simply because a story which would have made a tolerable book (the common run of stories) refuses to fill three books. Reardon's story was in itself weak, and this second volume had to consist almost entirely of laborious padding' (Gissing, *New Grub Street*, pp. 247, 161).

It is instructive to compare this specifically nineteenth-century publishing circumstance with the modern-day state of SF and Fantasy book culture. Fantasy publishing in particular, following the paradigm established by the genre-defining success of Tolkien's *The Lord of the Rings* – first published as a trilogy of titles, *The Fellowship of the Ring* (1954), *The Two Towers* (1954) and *The Return of the King* (1955) – is thick with trilogies; these are, in effect, today's triple-deckers. What is called 'middle volume syndrome' is a common complaint of reviewers and readers both: a version of the complaint Gissing makes: the first volume is interesting because it sets up the story and world, and the last volume is interesting because it pays off that story; but the middle volume too often is an exercise in literary water treading. If trilogies are far less common in SF publishing, it is precisely because the twentieth-century genre grew from different practical and publishing roots than did the genre of Fantasy.

Triple-deckers, despite their dominance, were of course not the only mode of book publication in the nineteenth century; despite the widely held belief (cited by Griest) that the British were not a book-buying population, some books *were* bought. In some cases, this is because the books in question were much cheaper than average, often because their production was subsidised by some organisation uninterested in Mudie's and other similar libraries. The most significant example of this circumstance was religious publication: a number of churches and religiously affiliated organisations provided subventions to enable the cheap distribution of Bibles – the Bible was the single bestselling book in the century as a whole – as well as tracts and similar works (Nord, *Faith in Reading*; Howsam, *Cheap Bibles*). This was not just a matter of theological non-fiction. It explains, for instance, why there were so many reprints of Bunyan's *Pilgrim's Progress* in this century. Bunyan's seventeenth-century piety justified the book from a perspective of Protestant proselytising, but it was its colourful fantastical touches that endeared it to readers, and the fact that it existed outside the triple-decker system licensed such non-mimetic elements (Owens and Sim, *Reception, Appropriation, Recollection*). *Pilgrim's Progress* was a book often read in childhood, and the growth in importance of children's literature across this period occupied another such marginal space: often illustrated, cheaper books, printed to be owned (perhaps given as gifts at birthday or Christmas), with strong fantastical elements, as in Charles Kingsley's *The Water Babies* (1863) or Lewis Carroll's enduring *Alice* books (1865, 1871). Indeed, the market for gift books, by definition a product primarily to be sold rather than lent by libraries, grew in importance as the century went on. The origins of this market can be traced to Charles Dickens's *A Christmas Carol* (1843), a volume specifically planned as something outside the usual run of Dickens's monthly serialised, three-volume larger novels: a book shorter, cheaper, to be bought and given away at Christmas. It is no coincidence that working in this shorter form freed Dickens up to venture beyond domestic realism – *A Christmas Carol*, of course, is a ghost story that includes quasi-SF time-travel elements – and the many imitators of this format followed suit in this. One example among many is Charles Rowcroft's

The Triumph of Woman: a Christmas Story (1848), in which an alien from outer space lands, via meteor, in the grounds of a German astronomer's house and falls in love with his daughter.

But there were two more important alternatives to buying triple-deckers from this period. One involved issuing novels in a series of cheap individual instalments, usually twelve or twenty. This was how most of Dickens's big novels were issued, and various other writers experimented with it – although John Sutherland (*VictorianFiction*) has called this form 'a bow of Ulysses that only Dickens could reliably string'. He adds that though this form 'served a valuable transitional function in mobilizing a nation-wide reading public before the full evolution of the fiction-carrying periodical' in the later 1860s, by the 1870s this mode of publication had entirely died out (p. 103). It needed the sheer popular appeal of a writer like Dickens to make this mode of publication work. Twenty instalments at a shilling each is, after all, a pound for the whole novel, which, when you add in the expense of having these loose pages bound into a volume at the end, meant that the mode was not appreciably cheaper than just spending 30s on a triple-decker. Better value for money was afforded by weekly magazines, like Dickens's own *Household Words* (published from 1850 onwards and, after a change of name to *All The Year Round* in 1859, through to and beyond the end of the century), *Chambers's Magazine* (which ran from 1832 through to the 1950s) or the *Cornhill Magazine* (1860–1972), which ran serialised novels and short stories alongside a variety of others kinds of journalism. These magazines were often cheaper than serial instalments – the *Cornhill* cost a shilling, but *Household Words* was only tuppence – and included short fiction and serialised novels.

Such magazines were, in turn, part of the explosion in British journalism occasioned by the abolition of the stamp duty tax that had been previously levied on newspapers and journals (deliberately so to make the popular press less viable, with the intention of suppressing popular political agitation and revolution). Advertisement duty was abolished in 1853, followed by newspaper stamp duty in 1855. The paper duty was removed in 1861, all of which made running newspapers or magazines much more cost effective. These so-called taxes on knowledge had never been popular, and their removal enabled a boom in cheaper publishing (Hewitt, *The Dawn of the Cheap Press in Victorian Britain*). Advances in the technologies of printing (especially of printing illustrations and coloured 'chromolithographs') also brought costs down.

New magazines, and larger circulation figures for existing journals, tracked the expansion of the reading public through the second half of the century. By the century's end, a huge variety of magazines and journals competed for the attention of – as noted – a greatly increased population of literate readers. Short stories became increasingly popular and were well suited to this new mode of publication: in the United States, the *Argosy* (founded in 1882, and later called the *Argosy All-Story Weekly*) and, in the UK, *Tit-Bits* (founded 1881, by 1890 it was selling 350,000 copies), the *Strand* magazine (founded 1890, and selling half a million copies by the middle of that decade) and *Pearson's Magazine* (founded 1896). In the words of Matthew Rubery, these late Victorians 'witnessed a boom in the volume of affordable books, magazines and newspapers produced to satisfy the demands of the first mass reading public'. Rubery quotes Wilkie Collins on this 'Unknown Public, the millions of readers of cheap print who were more likely to acquire their literature from the tobacconist's shop than the circulating library' (Rubery, 'Journalism', p. 177; see also Sullivan, *British Literary Magazines*).

These millions, in creating a new literary market, created a new literary culture. One character in Gissing's previously quoted *New Grub Street* (1891) ends the novel by making his fortune with a new magazine, *Chit-Chat* (Gissing's version of the real magazine *Tit-Bits*, mentioned earlier). This magazine is aimed at the great new generation that is being turned out by the Board schools, the young men and women who can just read, but are incapable of sustained attention. People of this kind want something to occupy them in trains and on 90 buses and trams. As a rule they care for no newspapers except the Sunday ones; what they want is the lightest and frothiest of chit-chatty information – bits of stories, bits of description, bits of scandal, bits of jokes, bits of statistics, bits of foolery. (Gissing, *New Grub Street*, p. 496)

It is the tonal condescension of this, as much as its articulation of a new fact of social history, that is so telling. Rather than acknowledge the validity of the non-mimetic and shorter modes of literary production, more fantastical and fractured, the older guard tended simply to dismiss it. As an iteration of this new popular culture, the literary establishment dismissed SF through much of the twentieth century, and some continue to dismiss it even to this day.

John Sutherland adopts a similarly dismissive tone when he sums up the broader changes in literary production across this period, addressing magazine publication in particular as 'a pervasive shift from gravity to frivolity' (Sutherland, *Victorian Fiction*, p. 19). It is indicative, in a small way, of a broader cultural marginalisation. Dan Jacobson is in many ways an estimable critic, but when he contemplates the genealogy of the modern short story he professes puzzlement at the 'mystery' of 'why English writers, who had at their disposal a periodical press which was at least as well-established as any on the Continent or in the United States should have been so slow to seize upon the possibilities' of the mode. He concurs with Walter Allen and V. S. Pritchett 'that Kipling was the first truly English writer to devote a significant proportion of his creative energy to the writing of stories' ('Jacobson, 'Ars Brevis, Vita Longis', p. 14). What, we wonder, turns masterpieces of the form like M. R. James's ghost stories, Conan Doyle's detective stories or – most relevantly here – H. G. Wells's superb SF short stories into the untouchables of this brand of literary history? But we do not need to wonder. It is genre itself, of course. The issue of the canonicity or otherwise of specific genres, discussed earlier, determines and, indeed, overdetermines critical reaction.

Latterly, critics have been more receptive to the merit as well as the importance of previously marginalised publishing spaces (Liddle, *The Dynamics of Genre*). Stella Pratt-Smith (*Transformations of Electricity in Nineteenth-Century Literature and Science*) notes how slowly the burgeoning form of the short story shook off associations of being a 'low' form, in part because, published predominantly in the periodical press, it 'was associated therefore with what was essentially a popular and relatively ephemeral forum'. She also argues that 'short fiction in cheap periodicals may have held considerably greater value to readers with limited resources in terms of finance, leisure time and literacy, for whom is frequently constituted the only form of literature to which they had access' (p. 111). Josephine Guy and Ian Small (*The Routledge Concise History of Nineteenth-Century Literature*) provide a wealth of references to support their assertion that changing the 'frame of reference' by which critics approach the period 'has led to the revaluation of an entire sub-genre' – they mean the once despised Gothic tradition, of course, but their argument is equally relevant to SF (p. 171). New technologies broadened the kinds as well as the amount of work being published:

> By the final decades of the nineteenth century the breaking of more technological constraints again forced the pace. The second great transformation of the book trades in this century was led by new technical processes ... rotary printing from 1870s, hot-metal typesetting from the late 1880s, and the use of lithographic and photographic

techniques at the very end of the century ... In 1841 some 50,000 men and women were employed in the paper, printing, book and stationary trades; by 1871 the total was some 125,000; by 1901 some 323,000. (Raven, 'The Changing Structure of Publishing', p. 283)

It is not only a question of book publication. The material culture of newspapers and magazines, which published a great deal of science fiction, crime and other marginalised literatures (most of Wells's and Conan Doyle's works appeared first in such venues) grew rapidly towards the end of the century:

The real price of newspapers and print fell markedly in the 1840s and then again, still more sharply, from the 1860s. Thereafter the newspaper market (and periodical printing) confidently advanced on the basis of the new lower middle-class and working-class market, sustained by new and cheaper raw materials for paper manufacture. By 1907 newspaper production accounted for 27% of the total net value of all British publications. (Raven, 'The Changing Structure of Publishing', p. 282)

That was just newspapers; taking magazines into account, the total share approaches a third.

In sum, then: the last three, and more acutely the last two, decades of the nineteenth century saw a comprehensive shift in the logic of publishing, book distribution, reading and therefore of cultural production more broadly defined. A combination of reductions in unit costs, greatly increased literacy in the general population, and relaxation of government controls produced a boom in publishing that in turn fed a new literary culture in which – to revert for a moment to the sketched-out SF canon with which I began my discussion – some SF writers enjoyed success on a scale that launched the genre as a popular cultural mode.

Meanwhile, literacy levels continued to rise and unit costs (unevenly, when one considers the impact of two world wars, but markedly nonetheless) continued to diminish throughout the twentieth century. But the window of book publication to which this present study is addressing itself closes during or shortly after the First World War; or if 'closes' is too absolute a term, then at least shrinks. Scientific Romance as a mode, one distinct from SF, is (as discussed earlier) particularly associated with a late Victorian and Edwardian aesthetic; by the 1920s Pulp was making the genre new in various ways. That is to say, the conditions of publishing shifted again, and the period of cultural production that produced 'scientific romance' shifted its logic again. The focus of this current study is on the material produced within that window, and its argument is that it is this body of work that has shaped the representational parameters of later twentieth- and twenty-first-century science fiction.

So what changed? On 1 January 1900, the UK established the Net Book Agreement, a policy that had first been proposed in 1890 by leading publisher Frederick Macmillan. This agreement pressured retailers into selling books at agreed – in plain terms, at *inflated* – prices. This was never law; it was only ever an agreement between the leading publishers of the day. But it was provided with effective commercial sanctions to enforce its reach. Any bookseller who elected to sell books at less than this 'agreed' price would no longer be supplied by the publishers who had signed the agreement. It proved an immensely effective tool. Although it was challenged in its early years from several directions (between 1905 and 1908, *The Times* offered its subscribers the opportunity of low-price book borrowing as a direct challenge to the Net Book Agreement, but this failed), by 1914, when novels were specifically included in the agreement, it had come to define the market, certainly in Britain at any rate.[12]

This is important to the question under discussion because the Net Book Agreement was in practice a move to brand books in terms of quality. The argument for introducing it at all was that it would enable better-selling titles to subsidise the production of worthwhile but less commercially appealing ones, and the justification for the publication of the latter sort of book was qualitative. Frederick Macmillan, the publisher who led the way with Net books, later recalled, 'it was important that the book chosen should be a good one because if the first net book did not sell its failure would certainly be attributed to its *netness* and not to its quality.' He chose to test the system with *The Principles of Economics* (1890) by Professor Alfred Marshall, since 'there was little doubt that this book would at once take a leading place in the literature of Economics, and it suggested itself as a most appropriate subject for the experiment we wished to try.' N. N. Feltes ('Anyone of Everybody'), who quotes this, comments:

> Here we have the beginning of an experiment in selling books as a new kind of 'branded goods'; rather than appealing to a known, limited market for a commodity-book ... to, say, the market for gilt edges and morocco bindings, Macmillan is here testing an assumed 'quality', a 'reputation-value', as a way of interpellating the 'unknown reader'. (p. 280)

Feltes notes that books advertised as 'net' in the early years of the scheme were one of two types: books 'on abstruse topics or in special formats or bindings'

---

[12] A contemporary memoir is Macmillan and Bell (*The Net Book Agreement 1899 and the Book War 1906–1908*).

which 'booksellers could not sell generally', or else 'books which by some sort of "reputation-value" may be hoped to interpolate an unspecified "class" of unknown readers' (p.281). It is this latter category that, once novels were included in the agreement in 1914, created the market conditions by which 'literature' was separated out from 'pulp' or 'genre' *on the level of reputation*. Feltes's example, a good one, is Forster's *Howard's End* (1910), a highly regarded, and in terms of 'the literary novel', canonical, work of 'high reputation' fiction. For the purposes of the present study, we can set this alongside the 1911 publication of Hugo Gernsback's first published work of SF, *Ralph 124 C 41+* (1911): a work of enormous in-genre influence and no discernible literary quality at all, serialised in a magazine, *Modern Electrics*, rather than published as a stand-alone novel (it would not appear in novel form until 1925).[13] We could let these two works stand as emblematic of the cleavage that increasingly opens between the 'official' culture of literary fiction on the one hand and the marginal, unofficial and often despised culture of genre fiction on the other as we move into the twentieth century.

To make my argument plain, I am suggesting that the Net Book Agreement, by applying price pressure to the cultural valorisation of certain

---

[13] Gary Westfahl (*Hugo Gernsback and the Century of Science Fiction*) notes the influence and importance of Gernsback's novel: 'throughout the twentieth century, as science fiction developed into a recognized literary genre, Hugo Gernsback's *Ralph 124C 41+* has repeatedly emerged at crucial defining moments' (p. 97). Westfahl repeats Sam Moskowitz's description of Gernsback as 'the father of modern science fiction'. On the literary worthlessness of the novel, see for example Brian Aldiss (1973), who describes it as a 'tawdry illiterate tale' and a 'sorry concoction', or Aldiss's later (1985) dismissal of it as 'a wretched crust' (p. 82). Aldiss objects not only to how badly written, characterised and structured the novel is, but also to the way it defines SF as nothing more than 'gadget fiction'. Westfahl is perfectly alert to the book's literary shortcomings, quoting Martin Gardner ('surely the worst SF novel ever written') and Lester Del Ray ('simply dreadful') amongst others.

kinds of books at the expense of certain other kinds, resumed the work that had earlier been carried out by the circulating libraries in the days before changes in the logistics and technology of production made the manufacture of cheap books a possibility. Mudie's, for example, assured its patrons that 'novels of objectionable character and inferior ability are almost invariably excluded' (Raven, 'The Changing Structure of Publishing', p. 285). Net Books performed a similar function half a century later.

Of course, the Net Book Agreement did not single-handedly separate out 'high literature' from 'popular culture' during this period. Other factors came into play, not the least of which was the increasing importance of English Studies as a university discipline. 'English' was a new branch of study, more or less invented by a group of academics at the end of the nineteenth and beginning of the twentieth centuries to create a shared culture of literary knowledge to replace the shared culture of religious and Latin/ Greek literatures.[14] According to Lise Jaillant (*Modernism, Middlebrow and the Literary Canon*), it was not until 1940 or so that 'flexibility was lost' in terms of literary categorisation, and it was not until after the Second World War that critics and academics more vocally 'called for the separation between "high" and "low" cultural forms' (p. 17). But although the thesis of her study is that there existed publishing ventures that bridged 'high' and 'low' culture through the 1920s and 1930s (her particular focus is the 'Modern Library', a New York series of cheap reprints that included amongst others work by Joyce, Woolf and Gertrude Stein), nonetheless she traces a post–First World War literary and cultural landscape increasingly divided along 'high' and 'low' lines.

---

[14] There is a large body of work on the creation of 'English' as a university discipline. See for instance Lawrie, *The Beginnings of University English* and Gildea et al., *English Studies*.

These features of book production and reception play a significant part in the way the canon of nineteenth- and early-twentieth-century SF developed. On the one hand there is a period, between the decline of the stranglehold of the circulating libraries and the new regime of maintaining the elevated price of books to ensure 'quality' (between the 1870s and about 1910) when advances in the technology of book production that made books markedly more affordable met a new reading public educated into literacy. On the other hand, newspapers and magazines (not, of course, part of the Net Book Agreement) increased very greatly in number, range and affordability.

This is the, as it were, sociocultural and economic frame into which the peculiar shape of the nineteenth- and early-twentieth-century canon of SF becomes more comprehensible. We see a sudden florescence of the SF novel in the 1880s and 1890s, just at the time that we also see the centre of gravity shift away from the form of the published novel to that of modes hospitable to magazine publication in the 1910s and 1920s. Those journals, illustrated on their exteriors by garishly coloured coal-tar dyes, the rest of each issue being printed so as to save money upon cheaper wood-pulp paper and decorated with black-and-white illustrations, are what gives this era of SF history its name. It is not the purpose of the present study to defend the Pulps, though, as it happens, that is a defence I am always prepared to offer due to their kinetic, fast-paced sublimity, the vigorous expressiveness of their metaphorical strategies and the way they laid down many of the conceptual and storytelling templates for the later genre. But the point about Pulps is that their mode of cheapness is always already marginalised, an association with shoddiness rather than efficiency or economy; and this bleeds through into SF as a mode, as a whole.

Our concern here is between these two markers, then: after the Gothic and post-Gothic mode of earlier nineteenth-century SF and before the rise to prominence of the Pulps in the 1920s, what we now call SF was dominated by that mode of writing known as 'scientific romance'.

The Conditions of Development 1880–1910

Roger Luckhurst's influential history of SF (2005) concentrates on the twentieth century and does not explore earlier instances of SF. This is a deliberate decision on his part, expressing his belief that it was only at the end of the nineteenth century that the sociocultural conditions were in place to enable SF in the modern sense to flower:

> These, then, are the conditions for the development of a new type of popular scientific fiction in the late nineteenth-century: mass literacy; new print vectors; a coherent ideology and emergent profession of science; everyday experience transformed by machines and mechanical processes, released in a steady stream from the work-benches of inventors and engineers. If, as Schivelbusch argues, the railway produces new ways of reading and new forms of fiction from the 1840s onwards, it would be expected that a conjuncture of a few short years that provides new magazines and book formats, phonographs or gramophones, cinematographs and kineto-scopes, and all manner of electrified urban spectacle would produce new literatures. It is what Friedrich Kittler has termed a 'discourse network', in which the 'network of technologies and institutions that allow a given culture to select, store and process relevant data' emerges in 'a distinctively new form around 1900'. Elsewhere Kittler comments that 'in the founding age of technological media' – dated to the years between 1880 and 1920 – 'the terror of their novelty was so overwhelming that literature registered it more acutely.' (p. 29; quoting Kittler, *Gramophone, Film and Typewriter*)

Luckhurst adds that 'it was in the popular writing that Kittler so steadfastly ignores that his novelty and terror were recorded, in texts that were nascent science fictions' (p. 29). At the risk of appearing pettifogging, I am going to suggest trimming Luckhurst's list of conditions of emergence, the clearer to see how scientific romance (as a mode in its own right) comes into cultural play. So although the broad point about the acceleration of both the pace and the scale of technological change holds, 'machines and mechanical processes' had been revolutionising human society since the plough and the sail; whilst both phonographic and cinematic technologies of cultural production begin to make their presence felt towards the end of the nineteenth century, it is really not until after the Second World War that these achieve the cultural dominance they possess today. From 1880 through to the 1920s, both modes were annexes to culture rather than central or shaping forces, with cinema burgeoning through the 1930s with the introduction of sound and, together with the rise of TV in the 1950s and 1960s, becoming the dominant global culture of today.[15]

Of more direct relevance to the florescence of scientific romance through the 1880–1920 period is the expansion of the railway network and the increased speed of travel these networks enabled. Moreover, the ancillary impacts of this new technology, as well as its core business of transporting people and goods around the country, had a direct shaping effect on the development of genre. The railway does indeed produce new ways of reading and new forms of fiction.

[15] William Howland Kenney (*Recorded Music in American Life*), notes that the biggest phonograph firm, Victor Talking Machine Company, had assets of less than $3 million in 1902, that record sales experienced various slumps over the next half century but that they 'took off in the 1950s', totalling $200 billion in 1954 and $3 billion in 1977 (p. 50). Necessarily truncated but insightful overviews of the rise of cinema are provided by Cousins, *The Story of Film*; Kemp, *Cinema*; and Nowell-Smith, *The Oxford History of World Cinema*.

In other words, as well as facilitating the movement of human beings (and freight), the railways were machines that generated new tranches of leisure. As they waited on platforms, or as they sat in the swaying carriages for the lengths of their journeys, passengers passed the time by reading. The market conditions, here, were new, and a new form of publishing and bookselling developed to meet them. In the UK, William Henry Smith expanded his father's newspaper vending business by opening booths at various railway stations, beginning with Euston in 1848, selling newspapers, journals and books – these latter generally cheap reprints of famous titles, known as 'yellowbacks' on account of the colour of their covers. The expansion of W. H. Smith's business model tracked the railway boom through the later nineteenth century. By the later 1850s, Smith had outlets in all major stations and had to open supply depots in Birmingham, Manchester and Liverpool to keep up with customer demand. The reprint business made Smith, in effect, not only a publisher but also one of the most successful publishers of his day, by virtue of combining publishing and distribution so effectively. The initial reprint deal in 1854 was with Chapman and Hall (publishers of Dickens, as well as Thackeray and Trollope) for 2s. reprints, although other deals were also struck as the company's success widened.[16] Smith also opened a cheap circulating library in 1860 (it remained in operation for more than a century).

In France, the publisher Louis Hachette, who had already by the 1860s become France's biggest publisher via an astute arrangement with the government to supply school textbooks, decided to imitate Smith's success. He

---

[16] See Eliot and Rose, *A Companion to the History of the Book* and Finkelstein and McCleery, *Introduction to Book History*. It was W. H. Smith who originated the nine-digit code for uniquely referencing books, known as Standard Book Numbering or SBN. This was adopted as international standard and was used until 1974, when it became the current ISBN scheme.

negotiated rights to establish bookstalls in French railway stations; by 1870, he had several thousand such stalls and shops. Like Smith in the UK, Hachette became a de facto publisher in his own right by reissuing cheap editions of famous novels (French originals by Honoré de Balzac, Georges Sand, Victor Hugo and others and translations of English titles by Dickens and Thackeray). Five hundred such titles were published under the rubric of the 'Bibliothèque des chemins de fer' (Library of the Railways), and the enterprise proved extremely successful in commercial terms, with the best-selling titles in the series selling in the hundreds of thousands (Parinet, 'Les bibliothèques de gare').

The impact of this combination of publishing, distribution, a newly literate and more or less captive audience and a drastic reduction in product cost was unprecedented in the prior history of literary culture. What Eileen DeMarco (*Reading and Riding*) says of France is just as true for Britain:

> Hachette's railroad bookstore monopoly stood at the crossroads of the economic, sociocultural and political metamorphoses of the nineteenth-century as both an agent and a reflection of these changes. Instrumental in the development of mass publishing in France, the railroad bookstore network was also the first major publishing enterprise to employ women on a large scale ... Hachette's railroad bookstore network [played] a crucial role in the evolution of French publishing in particular and the social, cultural and political changes of nineteenth-century France in general. (p. 11)

This context is of particular importance to the late-century explosion of interest in SF, or scientific romance. Three threads in particular are worth identifying, before more specific discussion of examples of prominent scientific romances from the era.

One is the question of mobility, its cognate mobilisation, and the formal embodiment in SF of the ways in which the railways – and the new railway literatures – reshaped the genre.[17] Early science fiction, or proto-SF, very often embodied movement or exploration: as when Lucian's second century AD *Ἀληθῆ διηγήματα* ('A True History') has a storm at sea lift its explorer-protagonists into space and deposit them on the moon, a journey repeated both in locational specifics and satirical mood by writers as diverse as Ariosto, Cyrano de Bergerac, Kepler and Edgar Allan Poe (Nicolson, *Voyages to the Moon*). Voyages to the moon have remained a popular theme in SF, but the mood shifts around the time we are discussing from satirical pseudo-allegorising or ironic comedy to a more serious engagement with the mechanics of the voyage and the scientific plausibility of what would be found there. This is not to argue for a facile mapping of rail travel onto space travel, but it is to suggest that the determining logic of a new reading public, a public often literally in motion, and carried by the most advanced technology of the day, tended to revert back upon the material context out of which it was being disseminated. Poe's *The Unparalleled Adventure of One Hans Pfaall* (1835) is a comic-satiric impossible voyage to the moon by hot-air balloon that dissolves into the hilarity of a hoax and confidence trick. Only a few decades later, this style of lunar voyage, which had been the default of the mode since Lucian, was no longer viable. Jules Verne's *Autour de la Lune* (1870) carries its explorers moon-ward in a device scrupulously explained in terms of possible technology. True, the moon rocket is fired out of a gigantic cannon, a method of launching that would 'really' kill its passengers, but otherwise the tone of the tale is conducted under the rubric of potentiality and undertaken for the sake of outward exploration rather than reversional satirical commentary. And, as Figure 1 from the first edition

[17] *Mobilisation* as a crucial feature of modernity; as such it is an idea developed by Taylor, *A Secular Age*. Roberts, *History of Science Fiction*, attempts to explore its importance to SF, and its connection with science-fictional mobility.

Figure 1 Illustration by Henri de Montaut for the first edition of Verne's *Autour de la Lune* (1870)

makes clear, what Verne's space vehicle itself most strongly resembles is, precisely, a train.

Though there has been quite a lot of research undertaken on the demographic complexion of the audience of late twentieth- and twenty-first-century SF, little specific work has been done on the late nineteenth- and early twentieth-century equivalent audience (Jenkins and Tulloch, *Science Fiction Audiences*). Studies of novel readers in general, without separating out SF fans, make the unsurprising observation that there was a major expansion in readership across this period. Brooks Landon (*Science Fiction After 1900*) argues that the cheaper 'dime novels' associated with the last decades of the century up to World War I 'were the dominant literary form in America [with] hundreds of millions of copies helping to create a mass audience'. He goes on to discuss one form of dime novel, 'the invention story', as the mode in which 'American SF found its first great audience and its clearest line of development' (p. 41). For Landon, the founding text of this mass culture was Edward Ellis's much-imitated *The Steam-Man of the Prairies* (1868). This story concerns a huge steam-powered robot man invented by a genius teenager called 'Johnny Brainerd'. Johnny uses the Steam-Man to pull him in a four-wheeled carriage all over America, having adventures wherever he goes. In other words, the Steam-Man is a souped-up or science-fictional reinvention of the core technology – railway travel – that was in turn closely implicated in the publishing conditions out of which dime novels, and the 'scientific romance' more generally, were created.

The second point I would make concerns the constraints of reading time, and the effect this had on the kind of SF being published. Older models of reading were predicated upon a small audience with a large amount of spare time and few other distractions. To read Richardson's *Clarissa* or Walter Scott's novels – the latter by far the most commercially successful of their time – requires the ability to spend long stretches of time immersing oneself in the work. Commuting times at the end of the nineteenth century were not so open ended: broadly passengers travelled for between twenty minutes and an hour (Webb, *Commuters*; Gately, *Rush Hours*). Practically speaking this favoured a reading experience that could be parcelled out into smaller segments: individual short stories or articles, or shorter books composed of shorter chapters. The mid-Victorian behemoths, the triple-deckers, marketed themselves in part upon a tacit sense of value-for-money: expensive books that at least provided many words for the reader to enjoy. The new, cheaper railway literatures not only had a much wider readership but also fitted themselves to the exigencies of those readers' timetables. Short-story magazines flourished: when the *Strand Magazine* began publishing in 1891, sales settled very quickly at the half million mark, an extraordinary figure (it was the *Strand* that published Conan Doyle's Sherlock Holmes short stories, as well as important early SF by H. G. Wells). Other magazines, such as *Argosy*, *All-Story*, *Black and White*, *The Idler* and (in France) *Le Petit Journal*, *Le Matin* and *Le Petit Parisien* – all of which enjoyed nationwide circulation of a million or more in 1900 – catered for this audience and very often published SF. Many of the most popular scientific romances from 1880 through the 1910s were either short stories or what we would nowadays call novella length (Wells's *The Time Machine* and *Invisible Man* are both, in effect, long short stories). It is rare for a SF novel of this epoch to run to more than 60,000–70,000 words, and examples of triple-decker length SF from this era are very rare. This in turn shaped the short story dominant modes of Pulp writing, which in turn, through the publication of cheap paperback 'fix-ups' of short stories into continuous longer narratives, shaped the SF book market in the 1950s and 1960s.[18]

---

[18] Classic examples of a 'fix-up' are Asimov's Foundation novels (*Foundation*, *Foundation and Empire*, *Second Foundation*), the content of which were published as separate short stories in the magazine *Astounding Science Fiction* in the 1940s, and later

The Extraordinisation of Ordinary Voyages

This mobility, these fantastic voyages – these Verneian *voyages extraordinaires* –
provide the most obvious ground of commonality shared by the various
examples of scientific romance of the 1880–1920 period. But we can say more
than this. What is new about these iterations of the age-old science-fictional
fascination with exploration is the way these voyages become increasingly
figured (as with the Vernean railway carriage–like moon rocket from *Autour
de la Lune*, cited earlier) in terms of the sorts of convenience and comfort
a commuter might expect.

Verne's Nautilus submarine from *Vingt mille lieues sous les mers* (1870)
ranges all around the world and from the surface of the ocean to its depths and
through all the world's seas. At the same time, it is fitted with every bourgeois
comfort and convenience, including an extensive kitchen and a lavishly furn-
ished dining room, a library, fine art paintings on the walls and several
collections of jewels. There is even an organ, upon which Captain Nemo
plays music to entertain himself. Similar comforts are elaborated in many of
Verne's travel machines and speculative technologies of motion. The huge
steamship, The Great Eastern, is, as the title of Verne's 1871 novel makes clear,
Une ville flottante (*A Floating City*), accordingly provided with all the con-
veniences of a city. *La maison à vapeur* (*The Steam House*, 1880) is, in effect,
a novelised tour of India, with Verne describing all the famous sites of that
country. Travel happens inside a house-sized conveyance, the comforts of

compiled into tessellated novel-length productions for cheap hardback and later
cheaper mass-market paperback sale in the 1950s. But there are a great many
examples of 'Golden Age' SF that follow this model. When Asimov returned to
his Foundation universe in the 1980s, writing new instalments that were specifically
planned as novel-length projects, the results were much longer and less successful
works, which were prolix and flabby.

which are described in detail, and which is pulled on its way by a life-sized steam-powered mechanical elephant called 'Behemoth'. The reader is offered the satisfactions of tourist travel without having to sacrifice any of the comforts of home.

In *Robur-le-Conquérant* (*Robur the Conquerer*, 1886), the titular inventor, in some ways an aerial Captain Nemo, has built a huge heavier-than-air flying craft, called the *Albatros* (*Albatross* in English), in which he traverses the globe. Again like the Nautilus, it is supplied with all the home comforts, including a library and lots of delicious food. *L'Île à hélice* (*Propeller Island*, 1895) is an entirely artificial island, fitted for luxury with splendid restaurants, entertainments and, of course, a library, which travels around the Pacific, driven by the huge propellers of the novel's title.

All these examples (and there are others from Verne's *oeuvre*) orient their extraordinary narratives around the comfort of the point-of-view character, and therefore the reader. And this has proved an enduring element in twentieth- and twenty-first-century SF. The bridge of *Star Trek*'s Starship Enterprise – the command centre of a vast spacecraft that can take you anywhere in the universe, and even backwards and forwards in time – is laid out like a comfortable sitting room. The captain occupies a padded easy chair and watches the cosmos on what amounts to a gigantic television screen. The bother of travel is removed (think of the show's 'transporter technology' that enables its characters to 'beam' instantaneously from place to place); the space travellers are styled as tourists on a luxury cruise. Similarly the BBC show *Doctor Who* reproduces this Verneian combination of exotic travel and creature comforts: the 'doctor's' spaceship, the TARDIS, larger inside than out, provides for all possible comforts.

Furthermore, this creation of, in effect, a bourgeois-comfortable commuter space inside the motion capsule is not in any way secondary to Verne's larger textual project. On the contrary, we can argue that it is the very ground of his appeal – the creation of 'safe spaces' inside his story, textual comfort bubbles, inside which the reader can safely explore the depths of the ocean, the far side of the moon, the centre of the earth, or any of the other locales of the *voyages extraordinaires*. Roland Barthes (*Mythologies*) posits this as the key to Verne's enduring appeal:

> Verne a construit une sorte de cosmogonie fermée sur elle-même, qui a ses catégories propres, son temps, son espace, sa plénitude, et même son principe existentiel. Ce principe me paraît être le geste continu de l'enfermement. L'imagination du voyage correspond chez Verne à une exploration de la clôture, et l'accord de Verne et de l'enfance ne vient pas d'une mystique banale de l'aventure, mais au contraire d'un bonheur commun du fini, que Ton retrouve dans la passion enfantine des cabanes et des tentes : s'enclore et s'installer, tel est le rêve existentiel de l'enfance et de Verne. L'archétype de ce rêve est ce roman presque parfait: L'Ile mystérieuse, où l'homme-enfant réinvente le monde, l'emplit, l'enclôt, s'y enferme, et couronne cet effort encyclopédique par la posture bourgeoise de l'appro-priation: pantoufles, pipe et coin du feu, pendant que dehors la tempête, c'est-à-dire l'infini, fait rage inutilement. (p. 75)

> (Verne has built a kind of self-sufficient cosmogony, which has its own categories, its own time, space, fulfilment and even existential principle. This principle, it seems to me, is the ceaseless action of secluding oneself. Imagination about travel corresponds in Verne to an exploration of closure, and the compatibility between Verne and childhood does not stem from a banal mystique of adventure, but on the contrary from

a common delight in the finite, which one also finds in children's passion for huts and tents: to enclose oneself and to settle, such is the existential dream of childhood and of Verne. The archetype of this dream is this almost perfect novel: *L'Ile mysterieuse*, in which the manchild re-invents the world, fills it, closes it, shuts himself up in it and crowns this encyclopaedic effort with the bourgeois posture of appropriation: slippers, pipe and fireside, while outside the storm, that is, the infinite, rages in vain.)

Wells, the other figure most strongly associated with the scientific romance, is in some ways a very different sort of writer than Verne: not only a generation younger (Verne was 38 when Wells was born) but the writer of a quite different sort of SF. The typical Verne tale figures a fantastic extrapolation of the possibilities of railway travel, moving its protagonists out of the ordinary and into the exotic and unusual location. The typical Wells tale works through the dramatic implications of some conceptual novum, or new idea, whose novelty typically erupts into a comfortable, bourgeois life. Such a novum might be the following: what if we had a machine that allowed us to travel in time? What if we could be invisible, or were invaded by aliens possessed of superior technology, or if we altered animals to give them the power of speech? Wells did occasionally write science-fictional *voyages extraordinaires* – *The Time Machine* (1895), *The First Men in the Moon* (1901) and *The War in the Air* (1908) are three such. More often, though, he keeps his protagonist in one place and moves the world around him, or makes the exotic commute into the protagonist's world. That is the situation in, for example, *The Wonderful Visit* (1895), when an angel comes to an English provincial town; *The War of the Worlds* (1989), when Martians invade England; or *When the Sleeper Awakes* (1899), in which the protagonist literally sleeps his way into a radically altered future, a sort of sleeper compartment on the metaphorical train commute to the year 2100. We could also mention *The Sea Lady* (1902), a story about a mermaid visiting Folkestone (itself a commuter town) and *In the Days of the Comet* (1906), in which a passing comet brushes the Earth with its tail, leaving strange chemicals which alter human nature and bring about a glorious new utopia. This is to confine ourselves to the scientific romances, and not discuss Wells's 'realist' or mimetic fictions, many of which have the same shape.

Nonetheless, these were texts generated out of the chronological gap from which scientific romance was created, and Wells's early SF reverts surprisingly often to the default of an affluent commuter passing the time. He does not supply his mobile characters with libraries, as does Verne; but it is striking to note how often newspapers and magazines crop up. Take, for example, the space craft of Wells's *First Men in the Moon* (1901), which travels to the moon by an antigravity drive called 'Cavorite'. It transports its two occupants, Cavor (its inventor) and the novel's narrator, Bedford, to wondrous locations and offers them marvellous vistas. But Bedford is more concerned with how he and his companion are going to pass the time during the journey.

'What have you got there?' Bedford asks. 'Haven't you brought anything to read?' replies Cavor. 'The voyage may last – We may be weeks! ... We shall be floating in this sphere with absolutely no occupation.' Accordingly Bedford obtains exactly the sort of reading material a real-world commuter would be likely to pick up from a W. H. Smith railway station bookshop: a copy of *Tit-Bits* and a *Lloyd's News* (Wells, *First Men in the Moon*, p. 31). Instead of enjoying the unprecedented views of Earth from space, gazing on the moon or exploring the possibilities of the journey's zero gravity, Wells's astronaut picks his way through the classified ads:

> I struck a column of mean little advertisements. 'A gentleman of private means is willing to lend money,' I read. Then somebody eccentric wanted to sell a Cutaway bicycle, 'quite new and cost £15,' for five pounds; and a lady in distress wished to dispose of some fish knives and forks, 'a wedding present,' at a great sacrifice ... I laughed, and let the paper drift from my hand. (p. 37)

Wells's *War of the Worlds* (1898) is about the destruction wrought upon southern England by the Martian invasion, their powerful 'heat-rays' and the red weed they bring from Mars, which aggressively colonises our mundane landscape. The story begins in Woking – another commuter town, a satellite to London and supplied with good rail connections to Waterloo station. The protagonist and narrator of Wells's novel then makes precisely that journey (although not by train, as the infrastructure has been smashed by the Martians). On foot he moves through western London until, in the city centre, he witnesses the death by disease of the alien invaders.

It is a testament to Wells's skill as a writer how powerfully he evokes the state of post-invasion England, after the defeat of the Martians and the reestablishment of human control. The world has, of course, been profoundly changed by the events described in the novel. Some of these changes are obvious: the red weed the invaders brought with them from Mars, the 'almost complete specimen' of a dead Martian 'in spirits in the Natural History Museum' and so on. I want, however, to isolate one artfully dropped-in reference in the novel's early chapters:

> I was at home at that hour and writing in my study; and although my French windows face towards Ottershaw and the

blind was up (for I loved in those days to look up at the night
sky), I saw nothing of it. (Wells, *The War of the Worlds*, p. 21)

At the point of writing this retrospective narrative, 'those days' here
referenced are long past: the night sky now a venue of fear instead of
wonder. A few pages later the narrator notes that 'few of the common
people in England had anything but the vaguest astronomical ideas in
those days' – pointing to a now in which everybody knows about the
solar system and the dangers it poses. Most striking of all is a sentence
towards the end of the opening chapter: 'People in these latter times scarcely
realize the abundance and enterprise of our 19th-century papers' (Wells,
The War of the Worlds, 22).

   The novel does not spell out precisely why the aftermath of
the Martian invasion should have so reduced the provision of news.
Perhaps the implication is that a shattered infrastructure cannot support
such things; but it is tempting to read a different significance into this
reference – that the disasters have cured humanity of its passion for news
as such. The news is a way in which we tell stories about ourselves
to ourselves, and one of the more radical things about *The War of the
Worlds* is, paradoxically enough, its basic suspicion of storytelling.
Wells's narrator falls in with a curate, whose narrative of the invasion
(that the Martians are agents of God's judgement against a sinful world) is
shown to be inadequate to events. Later the narrator meets an artilleryman
who spins a utopian future narrative with humanity creating a new high-
tech subterranean civilisation. But the artilleryman is shown to be an
ineffectual dreamer, his storytelling irrelevant to the grim reality.
The irony of this trope is that *The War of the Worlds* is itself, of course,
a story, a narrative we are invited to distrust. The narrator more-or-less
says so:

> Perhaps I am a man of exceptional moods. I do not know how far my experience is common. At times I suffer from the strangest sense of detachment from myself and the world about me. (Wells, *The War of the Worlds*, p. 91)

The narrator's quixotic mood is integral to the story as Wells tells it. Sometimes he is rationally dedicated to self-preservation; at other times strangely suicidal moods overcome him ('an insane resolve possessed me. I would die and end it'). Sometimes he travels over the landscape of the novel with purpose – to investigate the cylinder, to find his wife. At other times he moves passively, or even randomly. He is enough of an everyman to convey Wells's point: that the human species is inconstant, passive and easily overcome. He is a man in constant, restless motion. He is a creature of a new age of literal mobility.

The phrase 'literal mobility' should not lead the reader to believe that I am proposing that these writers of scientific romance did nothing more innovative than dress up actual railway travel and middle-class comfort into grander and further reaching new technologies. Mobility, as a literal feature of the new logic of work and life of the 1880s and 1890s (railways and bicycles played linked roles here) is the correlative of the symbolic mobility of new fluidity of social hierarchies, and the nascent possibilities of liberation from constrictions of class, gender and race. Wells took himself from a prospectless youth as a draper's assistant to one of the world's most famous and successful writers, the friend of presidents, philosophers and movie stars. In a sense the distinction I am suggesting between Verne and Wells – that in Verne's scientific romances characters tend to travel to the science-fictional novum whereas in Wells it tends to travel to them – also maps the shift in the centre of gravity of a changing society. At the beginning of the nineteenth century, and for much of its length, most were born, lived and died in the same parish. By the century's end, Britain and France were becoming places where people moved around a great deal. Instead of finding work on your doorstep, you travelled to where the work was. That social mobility is not only about physical travel, as on a commuter train. It is, as is argued earlier, about access to resources, cultural resources not the least. Everybody in Edward Bellamy's *Looking Backwards 2000–1887* (1888) goes out to work, and everybody works hard, though joyfully. But cultural resources come *to them* – Bellamy's nineteenth-century hero Julian West is astonished when his host, Edith Leete, invites him to a concert, only to discover that the music is being piped directly into her house. Much of the book actually takes place in the house's extensive library. Access to these resources is more than merely an element in the utopian vision of the future. It is the self-reflexive apotheosis of the book itself, the text that fashions the entire world of the future utopia for the reader.

Science Fiction's Visual Cultures

Hand-in-hand with new technologies of typographic book production were new technologies of image reproduction. Advances in steel engraving and lithography made book illustration much more affordable than it had previously been, such that illustrated books became much more widely disseminated as part of biblioculture. This has important consequences for the later development of science fiction and does so, I suggest, in ways that follow through on the argument I have been hitherto making about the role played by marginalised cultural spaces as seedbeds for the twentieth-century development of the genre.

Fully to draw the larger context would require more space than I have here: so, in brief – nineteenth- and twentieth-century SF was a visual culture in addition to being a verbal one. Lavishly, intricately illustrated books by Jules

Verne, Albert Robida and others generated a visual correlative for their science-fictional world building. Wells's genre novels were serialised in a variety of magazines and journals before book publication, always with attractive illustrations. In the early century, this visual component of SF texts became more pronounced: cheaper coal tar dyes meant that Pulp SF magazines could afford bright-coloured, dynamically memorable covers – a whole visual style grew up that codified and articulated 'SF-ness' in ways that are still immediately recognisable today: metallic robots, space ships, gruesome aliens, handsome space captains and scantily clad space princesses. Through the 1920s and 1930s, this visual culture grew in prominence and was joined by the development of comic books and such movie-making breakthroughs as Fritz Lang's *Metropolis* (1927), as much a triumph of iconic visual design and special effects as cinematic storytelling or characterisation.

This remained only a component in the larger logic of SF until after the Second World War, when a boom in (often cheaply made) SF movies and new SF comic books shifted the genre's centre of gravity towards the visual text. The tipping point in this larger shift was the prodigious, global success of George Lucas's *Star Wars* (1977) (see Roberts, *History of Science Fiction*). This gave a new commercial impetus to the creation of visual SF which in turn led to an effective domination of popular cinema by a series of visually spectacular special-effects-heavy cinematic franchises (the many *Star Wars* sequels, and the franchises associated with *Alien* and *Alien versus Predator*, *The Terminator*, *Blade Runner*, *The Matrix*, *Avatar* and latterly the Marvel Comic Universe movies) and TV serials (*Star Trek*, *Doctor Who* and many others), together with a widening cultural penetration by comic books, graphic novels and *bandes dessinées* and the rise of a whole new culture of video games, many of whose most financially successful titles are SF. This has led to a situation nowadays where SF is primarily a visual culture, and only secondarily a 'literature of ideas' or a verbal culture.

This development, or expansion of SF as visual idiom into the cultural space of SF as such, can be traced in a direct line back to the nineteenth century, and to the period under discussion, when a cleavage opened between the respectable 'realist' establishment arts of illustration and the less-respectable and more marginal popular modes.

Richard Maxwell (*The Victorian Illustrated Book*) has traced the rise of engraved illustrations as a feature of nineteenth-century book illustration. He shows in particular how the success of editions of Scott's novels illustrated by steel engravings based on the work of famous artists (J. M. W. Turner was only the most famous of the many artists

AT THE PIANO.

Figure 2 Illustration by Sir Samuel Luke Fields for Dickens's *Edwin Drood* (1870)

commissioned to illustrated the collected 'Magnum Opus' edition of Scott's novels in the late 1820s and early 1830s) led to the respectable centre of publishing, in both Britain and France, commissioning high-quality engravings for realist and triple-decker novels.

This coincided with a new esteem for engraving: Susanne Anderson-Riedel (*Creativity and Reproduction*) notes how, before the nineteenth century, the 'position of engravers at the *Académie* was inferior to that of painters and sculptors' with graphic artists 'excluded from the more advanced academic training programmes offered by the French government.' But, she notes, this changed after the creation of the *Section de Gravure* at the *Institute de France* in 1803 and 'the establishment of the prestigious Rome Prize' for engraved art (p. xiii). Through the decades that followed, certain modes of engraving became increasingly esteemed and valued. This was related to the rise of photography, which – although its dominant nineteenth-century use was for portraiture and landscape – also became a facet of realist and mainstream book publishing (Novak, *Realism, Photography and Nineteenth-Century Fiction*). Realist engravings were often based on photographic originals; photographic pioneer Fox Talbot promoted his new invention by publishing *Sun Pictures in Scotland* (1845), a book advertised as containing 'scenes connected with the life and writings of Sir Walter Scott'.[19] Richard Maxwell (*The Victorian Illustrated Book*) argues that by the 1860s and 1870s mainstream book illustration in Britain had outpaced that of France, although Maxwell does note the international successes, as illustrators, of Gustave Doré and Victor Hugo. But Maxwell also uses Hugo to gesture at a much more ambitious argument. As an example, he cites Hugo's 1874 novel, *Quatrevingt-treize* (*Ninety-Three*), which 'includes as characters three children, Breton hostages held by republican forces during the horrors of la vendee':

[19] For a much fuller discussion of this, see Wood, *The Shock of the Real*.

The children are kept in an old castle's library, located high up in a tower. Left to themselves they tear apart, page by page, an almost unique copy of a famous early printed book, lavishly illustrated; then standing at a window they let the pieces drift away. (pp. 396–97)

Maxwell finds in this scene a rebus for the way illustration becomes both fragmented and widely disseminated at the century goes on:

Famously in *Notre-Dame*, Hugo had formulated a myth of one cultural medium superseding another; as the Middle Ages waned, the book replaced the cathedral. *Quatrevingt-treize* add as supplement to this myth: the novelist suggests that, under the sign of modernity, the book itself must be reborn. (p. 397)

Though it is no part of Maxwell's argument, I am going to suggest that this new dissemination of the book as, in effect, a swarm of visual images is particularly tied to the development of SF as a specifically modern mode of art. This argument has its empirical side, since there was a boom in pulp and popular illustrations visualising fantastical, science-fictional and non-realist scenes and images towards the end of the nineteenth and into the twentieth century (some examples of this are discussed later). But it also has what might be called its 'theoretical' side, because of the way the *status* of these visual mass reproductions fed into the peculiar nature of SF as a mode of cultural production – as exhilaratingly inauthentic, vibrant, kinetic and ultimately as embodying the technological sublime it so often represented.

The key theoretical perspective here is Benjaminian, of course. In the words of Vanessa R. Schwartz and Jeannene M. Przyblyski (*The Nineteenth-Century Visual Culture Reader*), 'no essay has more of a foundational status in the history of visual culture' than Benjamin's 'Das Kunstwerk im Zeitalter seiner technischen Reproduzierbarkeit' (1935: the title means 'The Work of Art in the Age of Industry', but it is usually translated into English as 'The Work of Art in the Age of Mechanical Reproduction'). Broadly Benjamin argues that the widespread adoption of new technologies of lithography and photography, leading up to the creation of cinema itself degraded or diluted the 'aura' that had previously attached to the icon or visual image: the special quiddity or quasi-sacred quality associated with older modes of painting and sculpture, the roots of which lie in religious iconography. In this essay, as Schwartz and Przyblyski put it:

> Benjamin's intent was not to reduce explanations to technol-ogies, but to see in those technologies the crystallization and material embodiments of ways of imagining and experiencing the world. [Benjamin] frames the problems of visual culture as historical and material ones as opposed to universal and abstract ones ... A hallmark of this essay, which is reflected in many studies in the history of visual culture, is an interest in the relation between a period's visual technologies and its structures of understanding. Benjamin believed that every era has very special techniques of reproduction that corre-spond to it. (Schwartz and Przyblyski, *The Nineteenth-Century Visual Culture Reader*, p. 10)

It is possible to read Benjamin's destruction of the 'aura' of the visual image as a critique of contemporaneity, to recruit this essay to an argument about how the older modes of immersion in aesthetic beauty have been degraded into a vacuous culture of visual 'distraction' and deracination. But it is also possible to take his ideas in a more progressive direction: to see the evacuation of the sacral logic of transcendent 'presence' implicit in the aura in more liberating terms. As SF became an increasingly important cultural force through the twentieth century, the genre liberated all manner of aesthetic, ideological and indeed libidinal energies and set them to play in the context of a specifically *materialist* sublime. Though sometimes maligned as adolescent, it is precisely this raw disruptive energy, this kinetic force and directness, that makes SF so enduring.

It is, moreover, the degree of swerve away from strictly mimetic or realist modes that defines the genre as such. This is what Darko Suvin, attempting precisely to define the genre, calls 'the novum' or 'new thing': the things that exist in the SF text but not in the real world, and therefore not in texts mimetic of that real world (Suvin, *Metamorphoses of Science Fiction*). Suvin's novum is most often treated by critics on the level of the *content* of the text, such that if a given novel or film contains a time machine or a faster-than-light space ship or radically new concept of gender, then it is SF. But a more interesting approach might be the way the novum itself is so often a kind of reified or externalised embodiment of the *formal* logic of the structuring metaphor of SF, rather than just, as it were, a brute marker of difference as such. The structuring novum of the scientific romance is modernity, not in any totalising sense but much more specifically the modernity experienced by the new emergent middle classes.

To bring this back into the ambit of visual culture: it might seem obvious – and indeed is sometimes treated as axiomatic – that photography produces a more 'lifelike', more mimetic and more realistic representation than paintings, drawings and caricatures. In another sense, however, the very swerve introduced by the departure *from* specular verisimilitude entailed by those latter modes of art can, handled the right way, bring a greater vividness to the image. This is, of course, an observation as old as photography itself. Daniel Novak notes that it was almost a Victorian commonplace that photographs failed to achieve 'pictorial truth' and therefore 'failed to capture truth itself'. Novak argues that there was 'a wide-spread conviction that the photograph could not represent individuality, particularity and even the temporal moment' and produced only what Dickens dismissed as 'the ghost of art':

> Essays in photography in a number of Victorian journals, including Dickens's *Household Words* and *All The Year Round*, represented photography as a process that dismembered the body, while almost producing a photographic economy of interchangeable bodies and subjects. (Novak, *Realism, Photography and Nineteenth-Century Fiction*, pp. 7–8)

Exaggerated, caricature or purely visual imaginary art, on the other hand, can approach a counter-intuitive sort of quasi-mimetic vividness. It can flesh out the ghost.

The new literatures of scientific romance drew heavily on the resource of striking visual illustration to make their impact. Arthur B. Evans notes the 'amazing statistic' that there are 'over four thousand illustrations' in Verne's collected *Voyages Extraordinaires*: 'an average of 60+ illustrations per novel, one for every six to eight pages of text in the original in-octavo red and gold Hetzel editions' (Evans, 'The Illustrators of Jules Verne's Voyages Extraordinaires', p. 241). These illustrations, and others in the broader logic of the scientific romance, actualise the new mode of SF as such by pitching themselves somewhere between absolute verisimilitude and the satiric traditions of manifestly non-mimetic cartoonery. The parameters for a generic visual logic, the building blocks out of which a distinctive science-fictional style were to be erected, are to be found here.

Perhaps the richest source of examples of this is to be found in the work of prolific French artist Alfred Robida, whose *Le Vingtième Siècle* (1883), *La*

Figure 3 Futuristic tube train, as imaged by Robida in *Le Vingtième siècle* (Paris 1883)

Guerre au vingtième siècle (1887) and *Le Vingtième siècle: la vie électrique* (1890) figured in the SF canon with which the present study opened. These are all hybrid works, where verbal and visual textuality works together, although the balance between word and image is weighted more heavily towards the latter in Robida's output than is the case in, say, Verne. And Robida's visual texts are marvellous, textured with fine detail, intricate without being overbusy, and stylistically occupy a midway point between verisimilitude and caricature. The Robidan extrapolated twentieth century is crammed with technologies, and especially – as this study has been arguing – technologies of commuter

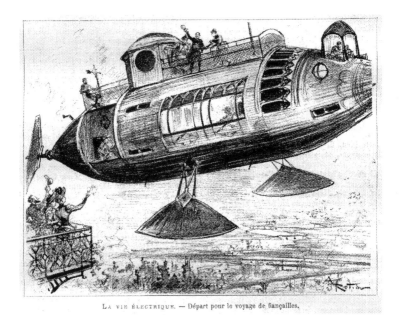

LA VIE ÉLECTRIQUE. — Départ pour le voyage de fiançailles.

Figure 4 Futuristic flying train, from Robida's *Le Vingtième siècle: la vie électrique* (1890)

travel and bourgeois comfort. Robida had a particular fascination with the possibilities of air travel, again extrapolating the middle-class railway passenger experience along the axis of technological futurity.

The converse to this, as with Bellamy and Verne, is that Robida's future matches its many advanced machines for travelling out into the world with the creation of an encysted bourgeois-space of heightened comfort and security into which the outside world is delivered by other kinds of advanced machines.

Figure 5 Robida's imagined 'téléphonoscope', from *Le Vingtième siècle* (1883)

In *Le Vingtième siècle* (1883), homes are fitted with taps that bring not only hot and cold water but hot *soup* into the home, and Robida goes one better than Bellamy's in-house provision of music by anticipating the invention of television by half a century or more.

This is an image about the future of the image, a self-reflexive engagement with modernity as a fundamentally visual logic, under which rubric other somatic pleasures – the bourgeois citizen's well-fed belly and cigar, the erotic titillation of the images he is watching – are subsumed.

Similar visual stylings are seen elsewhere throughout the scientific romance of this period. Brazilian artist Henrique Alvim Corrêa was commissioned to illustrate a 1906 French translation of Wells's *The War of the Worlds*. His work on this project was widely reproduced and became the novel's visual correlative in ways that influenced later film-makers. Wells himself thought the artist 'had done more for my work with his brush than I with my pen'. Once again, the style Corrêa adopts is at once photo-realistic and cartoonish; look for instance, at the googly-eyes of the Martian machines as they destroy a house with their heat-ray (Figure 6).

Or look at Figure 7, of the later portions of Wells's novel, where London has been ruined by the Martians who have themselves died. The dome of St Paul's Cathedral becomes a death's-head brooding over the city, and – in an additionally surreal touch – the windows of the buildings have all become gigantic eyes.

These eyes are another self-reflexive indication of the way these images construe the novum as visible, a scopophilic mirroring of the viewing eye back upon the viewed image. The contrast with those other Corrêa images that rest wholly within the more conventional logics of mimetic visual representation points to what this self-reflexivity adds. This image of a ruined Martian tripod, its dead pilot being devoured by carrion birds, is certainly beautiful in a bleak way, but it lacks something of the antic energy of the

Figure 6 Henrique Alvim Corrêa, 1906 illustration for Wells's *The War of the Worlds*

Figure 7 Henrique Alvim Corrêa, 1906 illustration for Wells's *The War of the Worlds*

Figure 8 Henrique Alvim Corrêa, 1906 illustration for Wells's *The War of the Worlds*

other images. It is less characteristically and energetically scientific-romantic in nature.

Some twenty-first-century visual science fiction special effects aim at a quasi-photographic verisimilitude of image, but most include some extra elements that revert the visual fiction back upon itself, either – as in the profusion of graphic novels, manga and anime texts, video games and the like – where a recognisably exaggerated or 'cartoony' element shapes the visuals or else by the inclusion of other deictic markers of self-reflexion. The sophisticated special effects of J. J. Abrams's rebooted *Star Trek* movies, for instance, include *ersatz* lens flare, as if actual cameras were filming the space ship battles in an actual physical space. The lens flare (widely remarked upon, and sometimes mocked, by fans) occupies, in a way, the same representational logic as the cartoon-like visual cues of non-mimesis in these scientific romance illustrations.

In contemporary steampunk, it is history itself that fills this role in the text: the technology might be the equal of twenty-first-century machinery in terms of what it can do, but the stylings, the visual fashion, is Victorian or Edwardian. And those steampunk stylings make a specific aesthetic point. The brutalist actuality of modern-day big-scale technological artefacts is softened with a touch of the more elegant design panache of the Edwardians; instead of the black, slug-shaped enormousness of a modern nuclear sub-marine, we are offered the beautiful intricacies of Captain Nemo's *Nautilus*: silver and art-deco-silhouetted, ornamented with attractive curlicues and stylish lines. In place of today's Pacino-in-Scarface vulgarity of vocabulary and manners, we have characters who speak in mannered Johnsonian or Dickensian phrases, who dress not in T-shirts and jogging pants but in exquisitely tailored suits.

It is, to repeat myself from earlier, the embourgeoisement of the technological sublime, a shrinkage of the alarmingly open-ended logics of

Figure 9 Grant E. Harrison's 'What We Are Coming To', *Judge Magazine* (New York, 1899)

extrapolated futures to the comfort and convenience of the new mobile middle-class citizen: the commuter, the home dweller. Domesticity is projected out-wards onto the cosmos, and that cosmos is modelled and reduced and brought to the domestic space. Grant Harrison's splendid illustration from the American weekly satirical magazine *Judge* encapsulates this essentially ideological logic in one image. What we are coming to, he suggests, is the compact folding together of the home, the city and all the new technologies of railway and tramline mass transit that bind that city together into one modular unit. It is, as is often the case with scientific romance, quirky and funny, but it is also eloquent and memorable. It is the perfection, at once exhilarating and existentially claustro-phobic, of the bourgeois Being-in-the-World that was, from 1880 through the First World War, increasingly the constitutive cultural logic of Western art and literature.

Conclusion

Part of the argument this Element has been advancing is that the canonical texts of SF construe technological advance by *embodying* this advance in particular, culturally determined ways. This is mostly clearly apparent in the way film SF has developed. In the techne of cinematic possibilities, SF movies *are themselves* what they represent. This is most obviously the case in the ferocious advances in 'special effects' that these films employ: SFX companies like Industrial Light and Magic or the Weta Workshop are more celebrated amongst fans than the actual film production companies that oversee the textual manufacture. Effects work with props, models and matt-screen; latterly, computer-generated and digital effects are a large part of what draws audiences to these movies. George Lucas's aesthetic is so intertwined with the fast-moving world of advances in the technologies of representation that he returns to previously released movies – films which, to reiterate, have already proved themselves extraordinary financial and cultural successes – to reshoot and titivate the SFX sequences. James Cameron initially planned to make his planetary romance *Avatar* in 1999 but delayed production for a decade to allow SFX technologies to 'catch up' with his vision (an earlier iteration of this phenomenon is Stanley Kubrick's plans for the movie *A.I.*, which stalled in the 1970s because the special effects could not create the illusion of a robot boy to Kubrick's satisfaction; the film was eventually made by Stephen Spielberg in 2001 – that is, when technologies of representation had advanced to the point where the project became achievable).

I do not mean to reduce 'SF cinema' merely to its special effects. But I do mean to suggest that cinematic, televisual and more recently video-game iterations of SF have today largely captured the global imaginary, and that they have done so because they both reflect back upon and in themselves *actualise* the technologies that have greatest purchase on contemporary culture and society. Science fiction movies often draw upon a reservoir of cultural anxiety and excitement (the two qualities very largely overlap of course) to tell stories about the potential for violence inherent in machines and the superior efficiency and reduced vulnerability of machines when compared to organic life. The older stories about robots and golems are given new, globally successful iterations in *The Terminator*, *Blade Runner* and *The Matrix*, more peripherally in *Star Wars* and *Avatar*. Or again: the near total interpenetration of modern life by technologies of communication and observation, from phones and computers to surveillance equipment, cameras, facial recognition, search algorithms and so on, inform a dystopian vision of the complete colonisation of the private by the public. This, again, is an age-old SF concern that is at the heart of novels like Zamiatin's *We* (1921) or Orwell's *Nineteen Eighty-Four* (1949). But a visual mode of art like film actualises as well as portrays the anxieties of visual culture.

Blade Runner, for example, works a complex set of eloquent variations upon eyes, seeing and being seen as it tells its story of 'replicants' – biological androids – who, though illegal means, hide in the plain sight of human society. The opening shot of the movie is an extreme close-up of an eye. The test designed to identify replicants involves a machine that observes ocular reaction to a string of questions. In a key scene the policeman protagonist (Deckard, played by Harrison Ford) examines a photograph under impossible levels of magnification to uncover vital clues. The lead rebel replicant (Roy Batty, played by Rutger Hauer) wants to meet his maker, Tyrell, in the hope that he can extend the replicants' artificially restricted lifespans. When he cannot, Batty kills him by squeezing out his eyes. Earlier, whilst tracking down Tyrell, Batty terrorises a minor technician called Chu, who specialises in making artificial eyes. In an attempt to ingratiate himself with the murdering replicant, Chu tells him: 'I made *your* eyes!' Batty's reply is more than an element in the filmic text; it is an eloquent encapsulation of the logic of SF cinema as such: 'Oh, Chu: if only you could see what I've seen with your eyes.' Cinema is similarly the artificial eye that enables us to see things we could not otherwise see, like futuristic cityscapes, space battles, aliens and wonders. In *Blade Runner*'s climactic scene, Deckard tracks Batty down but loses his fight with the (faster, stronger) machinic humanoid. Batty, though, spares Deckard's life. His own artificially shortened life is at an end; as he dies, Batty delivers one of the most famous – we could say, canonical – speeches in SF cinema: 'I've *seen* things you people wouldn't believe,' he announces. 'Attack ships on fire off the shoulder of Orion. I've watched c-beams glitter in the dark near the Tannhäuser Gate.' It is wholly apropos that these SF moments of wonder are rendered in terms of what is *seen*, and part of the movie's nuanced exploration of the borderline between blindness and sight is that these visions are denied to the audience, that *we* do not get to see them.

I have gone into *Blade Runner* at some length here in the hope of making a broader point. In its newer, globally reaching form as a visual literature, SF texts tend to both reflect and to self-reflect, to represent and substantiate the wider visual logic that increasingly determines modern life. I would wish to avoid being too neatly programmatic here: the canonical texts of today's SF may be primarily visual, but they are also (usually) rich and complex artefacts that do more than just iterate a scopophilic fascination and anxiety to do with questions of surveillance, screen simulacra replacing lived experience, appearance over reality and so on. But they do actually do those things, and the argument of the present study is that it is this that gives them their prodigious present-day cultural profile. To look again at how those Henrique Alvim Corrêa's 1906 illustrations for Wells's *The War of the Worlds* is to be struck how forcefully they emphasise as well as embody the ocular.

The main focus of this short Element has been later nineteenth- and earlier twentieth-century science fiction. I have attempted to gesture towards how large a part the visual text played in the scientific romance, and to indicate the way technologies of book production and distribution are reverted back within the very texts they enabled. Out of new commercial successes in story-telling that engaged with the technological pace of change, a style of text emerged that would, in turn, shape the mode – SF properly conceived – that developed from it. Later SF, though it expanded globally and became vastly more culturally diverse and successful, continues to reconfigure the icons of this shaping era of scientific romance.

The argument has been that the canonisation, in a literary-cultural sense, of a particular group of scientific romances at the end of the nineteenth and the beginning of the twentieth centuries, reflected a series of underlying shifts in the material culture of book production, distribution and consumption. More than this, the book has sought to argue that those material conditions, and the technologies that enabled them, were reflected back into the art that was being made. Technological advance found its most expressive cultural iteration in that mode of verbal and visual art predicated upon extrapolating the consequences of technological advance, that mode we now call SF. Put this way, it appears almost tautological, but familiarity with the genre's present-day tropes and conventions ought not to blind us to the fact that many of them derive not from the traditions of the Gothic but, quite particularly, from the scientific romances of 1880–1920. There is nothing inevitable about the genre's fascination with rapidity of transport, projecting outwards from the mass transit of new cities onto the cosmos as a whole; and there is nothing inevitable about a correlative fascination with bourgeois comfort. And yet so many of the rocket ships, time machines and star ships of mainstream SF combine both these elements. The culture of commuter trains and the reading spaces and windows-of-attention those trains enclosed figure in a thousand subsequent SF texts.

It is not simply a question of successful books directly influencing later imitators. Many of the texts listed in the putative canon at the start of this study are known today only to specialists, and yet they exert manifest effects on the later development of the genre. Chesney's *The Battle of Dorking* (1871) remains the template for the genre's penchant for alien invasion narratives (admittedly this influence comes down to us via Wells's *War of the Worlds*, which retold Chesney's story swapping out Martians for Prussians). Marie Corelli in her day sold millions of copies of books that wove together space travel and mysticism; though she is now forgotten, her peculiar blend is disclosed in the magic powers of the Jedi in the *Star Wars* universe and a hundred other examples. But usually the determinations are more straightforward.

In sum, SF came into cultural prominence at a time when publishing was remaking the book as a cultural artefact of vastly increased penetration. Scientific romance often reverts upon this fact in its narratives: Verne's

Voyage au centre de la Terre (*Voyage to the Centre of the Earth*, 1864) and H. Rider Haggard's *She: A History of Adventure* (1887) both begin with their heroes decoding ancient texts; Wells's heroes are often writers or journalists, as he was himself; Bellamy devotes a great deal of his utopian speculation to the future of the book and of libraries and to the dissemination of knowledge. And this material-culture ground in the quiddity of books, and the expansion of bookish knowledge, reoccurs on a cosmic scale in later SF: from Asimov's *Foundation* series, predicated upon the compilation of an *Encyclopedia Galactica* that is revealed to be the key to rescuing civilisation from destruction, to Douglas Adams's *Hitch-Hiker's Guide to the Galaxy*, an anticipation of the Internet as prescient as it is hilarious. In movies such as *The Matrix*, reality itself becomes a book, coded in strange tumbling glyphs that only adepts can read, and therefore alter, directly. L. Ron Hubbard (most famous for founding a religion called Scientology that is itself heavily indebted to SF) wrote a novel called *Typewriter in the Sky* (1940) in which reality is revealed as a novel being written by a hack author called Horace Hackett, an idea reworked by many writers, from Philip K. Dick, Harlan Eddison and Kurt Vonnegut, to composers of visual texts like Woody Allen in his *Purple Rose of Cairo* (1985), or Marc Foster in *Stranger Than Fiction* (2006), as well as the writers of TV shows like *Flashforward* (2009–10) and *The Good Place* (2017–18). In all these cases, a determining cultural climate of rapid expansion of book production, distribution and consumption has determined a metaphorical extrapolation of the book itself into the world. It is the sort of representational move, a sort of Big-Bang inflation of metaphorical signification to encompass everything, to which SF is particularly well suited.

The argument about trains I made earlier in this study has its particular iteration in this: later SF space ships are often more than just machines that can travel the universe that also enclose Verneian bourgeois in comfortable spaces (perfect environments in which to settle down and read a book); in many cases, the space ships of later SF become actual worlds. The figure of the 'generation star ship' has evolved from its earliest iterations as logical responses to the brute fact of the enormousness of the distances between stars into a major subgenre of SF itself, in which the commuter train – for the generation star ship is almost always headed towards some specific destination, rather than just flying without aim – becomes the whole world.[20]

That mundialisation, the systematic creation of whole worlds, has a name in the technical lexicon of SF fandom: it is *world building*. This connects with another, specialised usage of the term 'canon' within SF communities. Fans use the word to notate and resolve discrepancies in the world building that emerges in discussion of those SF texts that, like long-running TV or film series or multiple novels, elaborate their imagined worlds over time. For example, some of the aspects of the imagined future of *Star Trek: The Original Series* (1966–69) are incompatible with what is presented as the same imagined future in *Star Trek: The Next Generation* (1987–94), and indeed with the many other shows in that franchise. Faced with these inconsistencies, fans can either develop improbable explanations to reconcile them, or else – a simpler and more popular solution – select certain, consistent elements from the shared world of the stories as 'canon'. The *Star Wars* universe features not only in films and in television shows but also in a great many spin-off novelisations, comic books and video games. Only a small number of these latter are deemed part of the canon by the owners of the franchise's intellectual property; the rest are

---

[20] The first significant generation star ship story is Robert Heinlein's 'Universe' (1941), later expanded into the 1961 novel *Orphans of the Sky* (1963). As this subgenre developed, it produced a number of the most highly regarded works of modern SF, including Gene Wolfe's *Book of the Long Sun* (1993–96), Anthony Burgess's *End of the World News* (1982) and Kim Stanley Robinson's *Aurora* (2017).

deviations, grace notes, orthogonal extrapolations, whatever we might want to call them. This is not limited to science fiction: John Le Carré's spymaster, George Smiley, first appears in his early novel *A Murder of Quality* (1962); but Le Carré altered aspects of the character for his later novels, and although *A Murder of Quality* is still in print, and has not been disavowed by its author, it is not considered canon in terms of the 'Smileyverse'. But although an investment in ideas of canon in this sense is not limited to SF, it is much more prominently a feature of SF fan identity than it is elsewhere. And this captures something important about the genre: its valorisation of a type of internal conceptual consistency, its collective desire to as-it-were *mundify* its imaginative premises. To build a world is to actualise on a notionally global scale the logics this study has been discussing.

In a more capacious book, it would be possible to explore all the ways the forms of material production underlying late nineteenth- and early twentieth-century scientific romance became formally determinant of the later development of SF: the prioritisation of short stories and shorter novels; a copiousness of visual decoration rendered with a style that finds itself midway between the evidently caricatural and the photo-realistically mimetic; the social lineaments and attitudes of a new petit bourgeois reading public; technologies of travel; the diurnal logic of the commute and its attendant art of distraction from boredom; the magnitude of newly achieved speed and its corollary the apparent shrinkage of space. In each case we can see the repeated and reworked particular fascinations of later SF in germinal form.

I conclude briefly with that latter example: the geo-social reality of expanding cities and the experiential appearance of a shrinking world, extrapolated forwards and outwards in the literature of SF, gives us the world city, Asimov's Trantor, James Blish's cities in flight, George Lucas's Coruscant. Later SF is crowded with versions of the Grant E. Harrison's 'What We Are Coming To' cartoon reproduced earlier, and this city-as-world came to dominate the whole mode in the 1980s and 1990s as 'cyberpunk': the illustrations of 'Morpheus' (French artist Jean Giraud) for *Metal Hurlant*, the set designs for Scott's *Blade Runner*, the novels of William Gibson, the game design and storytelling of Masamune Shirow. But perhaps the most telling aspect for the vogue for cyberpunk is the way it morphed into, and was succeeded by, the steampunk mode discussed previously. To put it in a nutshell: steampunk is the return of the scientific romance into mainstream modern SF. The continuing popularity of this mode reveals something essential about the state of the genre today. SF, counter-intuitively enough, is often a mode of nostalgia for the future. Steampunk, by articulating nostalgia for the past, might appear to be a more straightforward, or less paradoxical, business; but in fact steampunk actualises nostalgia for the past *as the impossible future*. It offers a return to the base which the superstructure of contemporary SF is an expression. And, this study has been arguing, there is a reason why contemporary SF has this particular nostalgia for the late Victorian and Edwardian periods – that historical moment when the genre bloomed went from being a small-scale minority interest and began its expansion to its present-day status, as dominant world culture. SF embodies in itself the technologies of representation that it reflects back upon the world, as extrapolated fables, and for this key period in the historical development of the mode those technologies were to do with the new ways of printing, illustrating and distributing the marginalised stories of scientific romance. Through this moment in the history of publishing, what we now call science fiction metamorphosed into its modern form.

References

Aldiss, Brian (1973). *Billion Year Spree: the History of Science Fiction*, London: Weidenfeld and Nicholson.

Aldiss, Brian (1985). *The Detached Retina: Aspects of SF and Fantasy*, Liverpool. Liverpool University Press.

Anderson-Riedel, Susanne (2010). *Creativity and Reproduction: Nineteenth Century Engraving and the Academy*, Newcastle: Cambridge Scholars Publishing.

Ashley, Mike (2000). *The Time Machines: the Story of the Science Fiction Pulp Magazines*, Liverpool: Liverpool University Press.

Barthes, Roland (1957). *Mythologies*, Paris: Éditions du Seuil.

Bowley, Arthur Lyon (1900). *Wages in the United Kingdom in the Nineteenth-Century*, Cambridge: Cambridge University Press.

Butcher, William (2006). *Jules Verne: The Definitive Biography*, New York: Thunder's Mouth Press.

Cousins, Mark (2011). *The Story of Film: A Worldwide History*, London: Pavilion Books.

DeMarco, Eileen S. (2006). *Reading and Riding: Hachette's Railroad Bookstore Network in Nineteenth-Century France*, Bethlehem: Lehigh University Press.

Eliot, Simon (1995). 'Some Trends in British Book Production 1800-1919', in John O'Jordan and Robert L. Patten, eds. *Literature in the Marketplace: Nineteenth-Century Publishing and Reading Practices*. Cambridge: Cambridge University Press.

Eliot, Simon, and Jonathan Rose, eds (2007). *A Companion to the History of the Book*, Oxford: Wiley-Blackwell.

References

The Illustrators of Jules Verne's Voyages Extraordinaires'Evans, Arthur B. (1998). 'The Illustrators of Jules Verne's Voyages Extraordinaires', *Science Fiction Studies*, 241–70.

Farooq, Jennifer (2013). *Preaching in Eighteenth-Century London*, Woodbridge: Boydell and Brewer.

Falconer, Graham (2016) 'Provincial Circulating Libraries in Nineteenth-Century France: a Preliminary Survey', *Australian Journal of French Studies*, 190–204.

Feltes, N. N. (2002). 'Anyone of Everybody: Net Books and *Howards End*', in David Finkelstein and Alistair McCleery eds *The Book History Reader*, London: Routledge.

Finkelstein, David and Alistair McCleery (2013) *Introduction to Book History*, 2nd edn London: Routledge

Frederico, Annette (2000). *Idol of Suburbia: Marire Corelli and Late-Victorian Literary Culture*, Charlottesville: University of Virginia Press.

Furet, F., and J. Ozouf, eds (1977). *Lire et écrire: l'alphabétisation des français de Calvin à Jules Ferry*. Paris: Minuit.

Gately, Ian (2014). *Rush Hours*, London: Head of Zeus.

Gildea, Niall, Helena Goodwyn, Megan Kitching and Helen Tyson, eds (2015). *English Studies: The State of the Discipline, Past, Present, and Future*, Basingstoke: Palgrave Macmillan

Gissing, George (1891/1985). *New Grub Street*, Harmondsworth: Penguin.

Gorak, Jan (2013). *The Making of the Modern Canon: Genesis and Crisis of a Literary Idea*, London: Bloomsbury.

Griest, Guinevere L. (1970). *Mudie's Circulating Library and the Victorian Novel*, Bloomington: Indiana University Press.

Guillory, John (1993). *Cultural Capital: the Problem of Literary Canon Formation*. Chicago: University of Chicago Press.

Guy, Josephine and Ian Small (2011). *The Routledge Concise History of Nineteenth-Century Literature*, London: Routledge.

References

Heller, Agnes (2001). 'Cultural Memory, Identity and Civil Society', *International Politics and Society (Internationale Politik und Geschellschaft)*, pp. 139–43.

Hewitt, Jema (2011). *Steampunk Emporium: Creating Fantastical Jewelry, Devices and Oddments* New York: North Light Books.

Hewitt, Martin (2013). *The Dawn of the Cheap Press in Victorian Britain: the End of the "Taxes on Knowledge" 1849–1869*, London: Bloomsbury.

Hillegas, Mark (1967). *The Future as Nightmare: H. G. Wells and the Anti-Utopians*, Oxford: Oxford University Press.

Hogle, Jerrold E, ed. (2002). *The Cambridge Companion to Gothic Fiction*, Cambridge. Cambridge University Press.

Howsam, Leslie (1991). *Cheap Bibles: Nineteenth-Century Publishing and the British and Foreign Bible Society*, Cambridge: Cambridge University Press.

Jacobson, Dan (1981). 'Ars Brevis, Vita Longis', *London Review of Books*. www.lrb.co.uk/v03/n13/dan-jacobson/ars-brevis-vita-longa

Jaillant, Lisa (2014). *Modernism, Middlebrow and the Literary Canon: The Modern Library 1917–1955*, London: Routledge.

Jenkins, Henry, and John Tulloch (2005). *Science Fiction Audiences: Watching Star Trek and Doctor Who*, London: Routledge.

Kemp, Philip (2011). *Cinema: The Whole Story*, London: Thames and Hudson.

Kenney, William Howland (1999). *Recorded Music in American Life: The Phonograph and Popular Memory, 1890–1945*, Oxford: Oxford University Press.

Kittler, Friedrich (1999). *Gramophone, Film and Typewriter*, trans. by Geoffrey Winthrop-Young and Michael Wutz. Stanford: Stanford University Press.

Kolbas, Dean (2001). *Critical Theory and the Literary Canon*, Boulder: Westview Press.

Landon, Brooks (2014). *Science Fiction After 1900: From the Steam Man to the Stars*, London: Routledge.

Lawrie, Alexandra (2014). *The Beginnings of University English: Extramural Study, 1885–1910*, Basingstoke: Palgrave Macmillan.

Liddle, Dallas (2009). *The Dynamics of Genre: Journalism and the Practice of Literature in Mid-Victorian Britain*, Charlottesville: University of Virginia Press.

Luckhurst, Roger (2005). *Science Fiction*, Cambridge: Polity.

Lyons, Martyn (1999). 'New Readers in the Nineteenth Century', in Guilielmo Cavallo and Roger Chartier eds *A History of Reading in the West*, Amherst: University of Massachusetts Press.

Lyons, Martyn (2001). *Readers and Society in Nineteenth-century France: Workers, Women, Peasants*, Houndsmill: Palgrave.

Macmillan, Frederick, and Edward Bell (1924). *The Net Book Agreement 1899 and the Book War 1906–1908*, Oxford: Oxford University Press.

Marsocci, Joey, and Allison DeBlasio (2011). *How to Draw Steampunk*, New York: Walter Foster Publishing.

Martin, Andrew (1989). *The Mask of the Prophet: The Extraordinary Fictions of Jules Verne*, Oxford: Oxford University Press.

Maxwell, Richard, ed. (2002). *The Victorian Illustrated Book*, Charlottesville: University Press of Virginia.

Morrissey, Lee (2005). *Debating the Canon: A Reader from Addison to Nafisii*, Basingstoke: Palgrave Macmillan.

Nicolson, Marjorie Hope (1948). *Voyages to the Moon*, Basingstoke: Macmillan.

Nord, David Paul (2004). *Faith in Reading: Religious Publishing and the Birth of Mass Media in America*, Oxford: Oxford University Press.

Novak, Daniel A. (2008). *Realism, Photography and Nineteenth-Century Fiction*, Cambridge: Cambridge University Press.

Nowell-Smith, Geoffrey, ed. (1999). *The Oxford History of World Cinema*, Oxford: Oxford University Press.

Owens, W. R., and Stuart Sim, eds (2007). *Reception, Appropriation, Recollection: Bunyan's Pilgrim's Progress*, Oxford and Bern: Peter Lang.

Parent-Lardeur, Françoise (1999). *Lire à Paris au temps de Balzac*, Paris: Éditions de l'École.

Parinet, Elisabeth (1993). 'Les bibliothèques de gare, un nouveau réseau pour le livre', *Romantisme*, 95–106.

Pratt-Smith, Stella (2016). *Transformations of Electricity in Nineteenth-Century Literature and Science*, London: Routledge.

Raven, James (2005). 'The Changing Structure of Publishing', in Martin Drummond, ed., *The Organisation of Knowledge in Victorian Britain*, London: British Academy Scholarship.

Roberts, Adam (2016). *History of Science Fiction*, 2nd ed., Basingstoke: Palgrave Macmillan.

Rubery, Matthew (2010). 'Journalism', in Francis O'Gorman, ed. *The Cambridge Companion to Victorian Culture*, Cambridge: Cambridge University Press, pp. 177–94.

Ruud, Charles A. (1990). *Russian Entrepreneur: Publisher Ivan Sytin of Moscow, 1851–1934*, Ottawa: Carleton University Press.

Schwartz, Vanessa R., and Jeannene M. Przyblyski, eds (2004). *The Nineteenth-Century Visual Culture Reader*, London: Routledge.

Stapleford, Brian, David Langford and John Clute (2011). 'Scientific Romance', in John Clute, Peter Nicholls, David Langford and Graham Sleight, eds, *The Encyclopedia of Science Fiction*, 3rd ed., London: Gollancz, www.sf-encyclopedia.com/

Stapleford, Brian (2017). *Scientific Romance: An International Anthology of Pioneering Science Fiction*, Mineola, NY: Dover Publications.

Sullivan, Alvin (1984). *British Literary Magazines: The Victorian and Edwardian Age*, Ann Arbor: University of Michigan Press.

References

Sutherland, John (1965). *Victorian Fiction: Writers, Publishers, Readers*, Oxford: Oxford University Press.

Sutherland, John (1985). 'Must They Twinkle?' *London Review of Books*. www.lrb.co.uk/v07/n14/john-sutherland/must-they-twinkle.

Suvin, Darko (2016). *Metamorphoses of Science Fiction: On the Poetics and History of a Literary Genre*, Oxford: Peter Lang.

Taylor, Charles (2007). *A Secular Age*, Cambridge, MA: Harvard University Press.

VanderMeer, Jeff, and S. J. Chambers, eds (2011). *The Steampunk Bible: An Illustrated Guide to the World of Imaginary Airships, Corsets and Goggles, Mad Scientists and Strange Literature*, New York: Abrams Image.

Webb, Simon (2016). *Commuters: The History of a British Way of Life*, Barnsley: Pen and Sword.

Wells, Herbert George (1898). *The War of the Worlds*, London: Heinemann.

Wells, Herbert George (1901). *First Men in the Moon*, London: George Newnes.

Westfahl, Gary, (1998). *The Mechanics of Wonder: The Creation of the Idea of Science Fiction*, Liverpool: Liverpool University Press.

Westfahl, Gary (2007). *Hugo Gernsback and the Century of Science Fiction*, Jefferson, NC: McFarland

Wilson, Janelle L. (2005). *Nostalgia: Sanctuary of Meaning*, Lewisberg: Bucknell University Press.

Wood, Gillen D'Arcy (2001). *The Shock of the Real: Romanticism and Visual Culture, 1760–1860*, Basingstoke: Palgrave.

Woods, Robert (2009). *The Demography of Victorian England and Wales*, Cambridge: Cambridge University Press.

Cambridge Elements

Publishing and Book Culture

Series Editor
Samantha Rayner
University College London

Samantha Rayner is a Reader in UCL's Department of Information Studies. She is also Director of UCL's Centre for Publishing, co-Director of the Bloomsbury CHAPTER (Communication History, Authorship, Publishing, Textual Editing and Reading) and co-editor of the Academic Book of the Future BOOC (Book as Open Online Content) with UCL Press.

Associate Editor
Rebecca Lyons
University of Bristol

Rebecca Lyons is a Teaching Fellow at the University of Bristol. She is also co-editor of the experimental BOOC (Book as Open Online Content) at UCL Press. She teaches and researches book and reading history, particularly female owners and readers of Arthurian literature in fifteenth- and sixteenth-century England, and also has research interests in digital academic publishing.

Advisory Board

Simone Murray, Monash University
Claire Squires, University of Stirling
Andrew Nash, University of London

Leslie Howsam, Ryerson University
David Finkelstein, University of Edinburgh

Alexis Weedon, University of Bedfordshire

Alan Staton, Booksellers Association

Angus Phillips, Oxford International Centre for Publishing

Richard Fisher, Yale University Press

John Maxwell, Simon Fraser University

Shafquat Towheed, The Open University

Jen McCall, Emerald Publishing

ABOUT THE SERIES

This series aims to fill the demand for easily accessible, quality texts available for teaching and research in the diverse and dynamic fields of Publishing and Book Culture. Rigorously researched and peer-reviewed Elements will be published under themes, or 'Gatherings'. These Elements should be the first check point for researchers or students working on that area of publishing and book trade history and practice: we hope that, situated so logically at Cambridge University Press, where academic publishing in the UK began, it will develop to create an unrivalled space where these histories and practices can be investigated and preserved.

Cambridge Elements

Publishing and Book Culture
Publishing the Canon

Gathering Editor: Leah Tether

Leah Tether is a Reader in Medieval Literature and Digital Cultures at the University of Bristol. Her research is on historical publishing practices from manuscript to digital, and she has a special interest in Arthurian literature of the Middle Ages. She is the author of *Publishing the Grail in Medieval and Renaissance France* (2017).

ELEMENTS IN THE GATHERING

Contingent Canons: African Literature and the Politics of Location
Madhu Krishnan

Publishing the Science Fiction Canon: The Case of Scientific Romance
Adam Roberts

Printed in the United States
By Bookmasters